101 Poems, 35 Quotes, 52 Short Verses

by
Hubert Winston Anderson

authorHOUSE®

AuthorHouse™
1663 Liberty Drive, Suite 200
Bloomington, IN 47403
www.authorhouse.com
Phone: 1-800-839-8640

© 2007 Hubert Winston Anderson. All rights reserved.

No part of this book may be reproduced, stored in a retrieval system, or transmitted by any means without the written permission of the author.

First published by AuthorHouse 7/26/2007

ISBN: 978-1-4343-1836-7 (sc)

Printed in the United States of America
Bloomington, Indiana

This book is printed on acid-free paper.

* Preface *

Poems ... Verses ... Quotes ... Various titles.

* Introduction *

To all readers of this book, please note my name is written below, and I was born in a little district called Oxford in the parish of St. Mary, Jamaica in the West Indies.

I am one of six children that were four brothers including myself and two lovely sisters, from a wonderful and lovely mother and father, whom I believed were the very best parents created by God in the world. They were not rich in cash, but for sure they were more than rich in God's wonderful blessings of good ideas, instructions, guidance and directions for their children, and even for other children.

I recalled as we grew up with our parents, and in all life's beautiful ways, they were always giving us the best and most caring advice as to how we must conduct ourselves in our future lives as we marched into our responsibilities. Those things we all knew today, as their instructions and advices had proven to be more than correct as we took on responsibilities of our own. I recalled they told us never to steal, or be dishonest with anyone in any way, never to tell lies, or get ourselves involved in any problems with the law, never to covet anyone for anything they have got, never to be involved in gangs and never to get ourselves involved in other people's private business.

They advised us to mind our own business at all times, to always look up and aim high with good ambition as our goal. Today we all did not reach our goal or to the heights of greatness we had hoped for, but still we are not down, out and cold. Thank God we can still hold our heads in high esteem, and still be happy regardless of what we have achieved. My father gave us these words to keep in mind as we go through life, and for sure I never forget them. Writing makes me a correct and exact person; Reading will make us knowledgeable; and Conference will make us, fully up- right and fearless in all our goals. These words were perfect for us in all our everyday tasks, so maybe those words helped and inspired me at this time to be able to write these poems, so thanks a lot my wonderful father.

Adhering to my lovely parent's advices, and as I tread along life's difficult, discouraging and tough pathway, I kept reading and writing a lot as I always enjoyed doing. Sometime ago I decided to try my pen and ink in writing something, so immediately I went about my thoughts and ideas of writing this book of poems.

Please note carefully that I am not a trained or experienced writer, although in my mind and heart, I felt as if was a born writer of my own ideas and of other things. I really hope you will find something in this book that could be very interesting and satisfying to your desires. Thanks.

Hubert Winston Anderson

* Contents *

101 Poems

(1) My Writings. 1
(2) My relatives. 1
(3) My school days. 2
(4) Months. 3
(5) Jamaica. 3
(6) Leaving home. 4
(7) This world. 5
(8) Friends. 6
(9) Live nice in this world. 6
(10) My family. 6
(11) Mother. 7
(12) What shall I do? 8
(13) Friendship. 8
(14) Away from home. 9
(15) My way of life. 10
(16) Looking afar. 11
(17) I will be home. 11
(18) Come Jamaica way. 12
(19) My toiling years. 13
(20) My beautiful hours. 14
(21) My visit to Jamaica. 16
(22) Love. 17
(23) The loss of a loved one. 17
(24) Dreams. 18
(25) My daughter. 19
(26) A loved one lost. 20
(27) Live right. 21
(28) Never grudge. 22
(29) Ambition. 22
(30) Tomorrow. 23
(31) Hyde Park. (Speaker's corner, London England.) 24
(32) Spring time. 25
(33) Young Street. (Toronto) 25

(34) How Lucky.	26
(35) Summertime.	27
(36) Our love affair.	28
(37) Winter season...... (Canada)	29
(38) Open your heart.	30
(39) Dark night in Toronto. (In Toronto.)	31
(40) Martin Luther King.	32
(41) Wars.	33
(42) Work.	34
(43) My wedding knot.	35
(44) Debt.	36
(45) Drugs.	37
(46) Taxis.	38
(47) Politicians.	38
(48) Canada.	39
(49) Beggars.	40
(50) The brave.	41
(51) The alphabet.	42
(52) The gambler.	43
(53) Prejudice or racism.	43
(54) The cyclist.	44
(55) Never disregard.	45
(56) Aim high.	46
(57) Unity.	47
(58) Jealousy.	48
(59) Let's not fear.	49
(60) I wish.	49
(61) Seven negatives of life.	50
(62) Night out.	51
(63) My song. (wishes of life")	52
(64) My early walk.	53
(65) Loneliness.	53
(66) Where will I turn?	55
(67) Let's not forget.	55
(68) Women.	56
(69) The day I met you.	57
(70) A lover	59

(71) Our secret togetherness 60
(72) Adore me. 61
(73) Music to me. 62
(74) Dogs. 63
(75) Glory days. 64
(76) The lost lover. (My dream.) 65
(77) Never look back. 66
(78) A secret. 67
(79) Young and the old. 67
(80) Rich and poor. 68
(81) The poinsettias. 69
(82) Never walk away from me. 70
(83) The cab driver. 71
(84) Weapons of war. 71
(85) I Will Wait. 72
(86) A woman. 73
(87) I remember. 74
(89) Poverty. 75
(89) Fall season (Canada) 76
(90) Snow. 76
(91) At the end of a love affair. 77
(92) Love me. 78
(93) Reach out 79
(94) Yearning for love 80
(95) Thanks for waiting. 81
(96) How I see love. 82
(97) Discouragements 84
(98) Be happy with yourself. 85
(99) War remembrance. 86
(100) The warmth, of a lover. 87
(101) Burdens in this life. 88

35 Quotes
"Thirty five quotes" 93

52 Short Verses
Double alphabet in short verses. 101

xi

101 Poems

(1) My Writings.

I was never trained to be a writer,
In just the way I was never a baby sitter.
Comments and criticism are welcome,
And that is expected from some.

My words and writings are my own thoughts,
By no one had I been ever taught.
So read and digest, as sometimes you may laugh,
But while I was writing, I never felt any wrath.

These lines are subjects for comments and criticism,
But, read keenly, there are lots of rhythms.
So, read, enjoy and have some fun,
With the light inside and outside in the sun.

It's the love I really have for words,
For sure they are better than swinging a sword.
So readers, I am very happy with myself,
Read all my friends, before stocking them to the shelves.

....

(2) My relatives.

Mother and father, God bless you both, for sure,
For we as your children always cared.
Born and grown in lovely St. Mary town,
There you both took care of us as your own.

We are a lovely and Godly united family,
So I knew we are truly blessed from eternity.
Depressed moments we shared at times,
But we emerged from them without any crimes.

A family brought up to love and unite,
Each and everyday, God made so bright.

Hungry at times, but were still filled with life,
Just the way we were happy flying our kites.

A family, true in spirit heart and love,
God seemed to create us more like doves.
Sure, we never differ from our love and unity,
And never will do, even after eternity.

....

(3) My school days.

I remember my early morn awakenings,
I had to do so, just for my schooling.
I recalled the wonderful and warm days,
We together had lots and lots of plays.

My school days, in every minute were just great,
Although through the years I did not accomplish my feat.
But I still remembered all my friends and school chums,
And a few of them who were really bums.

Together we enjoyed lovely games of cricket and baseball,
Girls and boys together we played softball.
Yes! We were a wonderful bunch of friends,
And today, many of us still continue the trend.

The game of marbles we enjoyed at play,
And, sometimes we played on the road or in the clay.
It was a game of real fun, indoors or outdoors,
And it didn't matter even if the rain pours.

I remembered our church minister, a wonderful preacher,
A school Principal name Zetta Scarlet, an awesome teacher.

I remembered Fay, Dulcie, Yvonne, Pamela and Veronica,
Those classmates were charming and sweet like icicles.

I remembered the lovely togetherness we all shared,
And certainly there were nothing we ever feared.
I recalled those school days with some fuss and trust,
So, with me I would never let those memories rust.

....

(4) Months.

January,	cold, but not too bad,
February,	snow, that made the children glad.
March,	here comes the rain and wind,
April,	for sure, sometimes it is a little more kind.
May,	we till the land and sow the seeds,
June,	brings the warmth, and even men out in tweeds.
July,	all trees and shrubs are filled with leaves again,
August,	sometimes very dry, sometimes hot without any rain,
September,	harvest time from the May seeds grown,
October,	we see the vegetables all overgrown.
November,	cold again, but everyone seems to be fine,
December,	oh! It's glad tidings, because it's Christmas time.

....

(5) Jamaica.

Jamaica the island that I truly loved,
An island where the Arawaks came and settled
But once Columbus came, they removed,
Why? He offered them not much but just a little.

Born there, lived there, but then one become anxious to leave,
But after leaving it, one sometimes really grieved.
Jamaica is a land with beautiful treasures,
An island for lovers and an island filled with pleasures.

Jamaicans, do not ever crave for the world outside,
Work hard, relax, be content, so one day you could decide,
That wherever you traveled to, from this lovely island,
You could never find another so grand.

Be happy all Jamaicans, and enjoy your lovely island,
There's no better place for love, laughs and joys in the sands.
This is Jamaica, where we all called our home,
Here we find many things to do, and many places to roam

....

(6) Leaving home.

The time had come to leave my home,
Out into the world to work, admire, enjoy and roam.
Leaving the loving arms of my mother and father,
Just to be away from home and in a different weather.

Behind I left my brothers and sisters,
Out and far away, reminiscing to myself in silent whispers.
Of the love we shared while we were together,
Now I am far away, wishing that I could feel much better.

The awesome togetherness we shared, morn, noon and night,
Was something we all did, out-right,
Now the parting tears began to flow,
As my mother prayed quietly, while my father sewed.

Its goodbye mother, father, brothers, sisters and uncles,
All packed now, my suitcase, briefcase and my bungles.

Sad to leave you all behind, but do not pine,
God's great love will bring me back many times.

....

(7) This world.

This world is a place of beauty and satisfaction,
That was so from the day of resurrection.
Where beauty aught to be found in abundance,
Although there are many who sit back in reluctance.

The sun, the moon and the stars,
What better grandeur, could be seen from afar.
Without them life would never be so wonderful,
Love them, admire them and be very careful.

This world possessed each and everyone's needs,
Only that some are so fully absorbed in greed.
A world where many are weary, some very happy and some so sad,
That sometimes caused many to go really mad.

This world, so wonderful for animals, trees, insects and human beings,
What better place where one to rest eat, walk and lean?
But, within this spacious and lovely abode,
Where there are lovely things to see and enjoy before we fades.

This world with its pleasantry all around,
There is no better place to feel so sound.
Although filled with noise, pollution, wars and troubles,
It's still a better place than lying in the rubbles.

This beautiful world, a place for all of us,
Let's love it, cherish it, and enjoy it, as we pray and trust.
For this world is truly so great and prosperous,
In which we must admire, cherish and be very conscious.

(8) Friends.

Friends, are you really my friends?
Well! Outstretched your arms, and lend me a hand.
My faith in you will be forever always,
Even in disappointment and disarrays.

A friend true in spirit heart and mind,
A good friend is always trustworthy and kind.
A friend, true and faithful, who never pretends,
Without any doubt, a clean friendship never ends.

(9) Live nice in this world.

Let's live nice together in this hemisphere,
Before we all begin to wear and tear.
It's the best life in this world to live and to enjoy,
And we should never worry fuss or fear.

Let's live nice and forget all the bad deeds,
And with that we all could sow good seeds.
Seeds that would flourish, long, long after this good life,
And in the way that would help to avoid all fuss and fights.

(10) My family.

Leaving home, parents and kins,
To the outside world I wondered tall and thin.

Wondering if I would ever see their faces again,
Soon I left the airport and into the first British train.

Out into the world, I found a lovely girl,
Her tenderness and warmth placed me into a twirl.
Love blossomed, and romance enjoyed with lots of pride,
And very soon she became my bride.

Born from her, are three lovely children,
Sweet they are, as reading the book of revelation.
Here they are growing wise and intelligent,
Learning a lot, they made their future very pleasant.

My lovely family has provided one another with love and cheers,
And together we model ourselves without any fears.
For sure, there is true love in this family tie,
That will only give happiness, and no need to cry.

....

(11) Mother.

Our awesome mother, so loving and tender,
Great cares to her children, she always rendered.
Very, very wise and sensitive towards her children,
To her, we were worth more than a billion.

A mother who adores, loved and cares,
A mother who did our clothes with real cares,
Just as she prepared our food or lovely dishes,
And sometimes she does with lots of fishes.

It's great to have a real lovely mom,
Who to play with, talk with, and have lots of fun.
Without a wonderful mother, life could be really dim,
That at times could wear you down very slim.

A mother who grew her children so nice and lovingly,
Mother, you directed her children into their new beginning.
A mother who showed lots of love, cares and sometimes tears,
Oh mother, we knew all you have to bare.

A mother, so sweet, lovely and loving,
She was so wonderful to hug, on one's home coming.
A good mother, blessed by the almighty,
Would always be there shining so brightly.

....

(12) What shall I do?

What must I do while the lights are shining?
That is so wonderful from the beginning.
What will I do when the darkness overshadows me?
For I know I cannot even move as a flea.

What will I do, when the hour comes and my eyes are closed?
From where I will not, again be aroused.
Maybe life will be happier, or maybe a bore,
For that will be the moment, when I could not say, what will I do?

....

(13) Friendship.

Friendship is something we all need in this life,
It's good to life, as the taste of a sweet apple bite.
Without friends, our lives could be hopeless,
And at times could make our lives, listless.

Friendship, of human, insects, animals and birds,
Must always be first, and never placed third.

Friendship, brings to us a lot of remembrance,
Even if it happened by coincidence.

Good friendship, can give us peace and content,
So, never refuse to accept a friend, and never relent.
Let's all accept each other as one, and forget our color or creed,
And through this lovely life, we would be sowing good seeds.

This world is so wonderful, and so sweet,
And whether we accomplish or not, our feat,
Let's bind ourselves in true friendship and love,
In the way we admired a pond, with the paddling ducks.

....

(14) Away from home.

Living away from my island of birth,
Is like being in the sky, and away from the earth,
Wondering why I am away and here,
Pondering too, whether it's better to be here or there.

The dreams I had, and did wondered about,
Appear to me, to be somehow in doubt.
But come what may, I will struggle on,
Even to do so with a shaky hand.

This outside world, is not my real home,
But to many others, it's like a throne.
I just can't forget my hometown, my loved ones and my roots,
There was happiness, as I walked in new boots.

Away from home, and with relatives out of site,
In no way my heart and my mind can ever be al-right.
But in life I always had the desire to try something new,
And that was why I had to say adieu.

Being away from home is very sad to swallow,
But at times your mind and heart you have to follow.
I realized that being away from home, I sometimes become depressed,
But with faith and confidence, I would always be back, and refreshed.

....

(15) My way of life.

In a family of six I was born,
And our parents brought us up, with lots of strain.
And, as the years went by, out into the world I ventured,
Where I roamed the world, and enjoy new adventures.

Along life's way I think and aimed for a lot,
Like marksmen on the range aiming their shots.
At times my mind became bundled with many plans,
When I stroll on the beach, and saw people getting their sun tan.

I often asked myself, what will I be?
While pursuing many ideas, knowing I am free.
To be a lawyer, a photographer, a writer or actor,
But in no way I wanted to be a doctor.

I love beautiful things, and enjoyed love scenes,
Just the way I loved having good dreams.
My relatives and my family I adore very much,
And my friends, I will always give a friendly touch.

I admire the lovely people of all nations,
For we are all God's chosen creation.
So let's give at all times, a warm and tender smile,
To all, even if they are as far as a mile.

Minding my own private affairs, I always prefer,
Other's private lives, I do not ever refer.

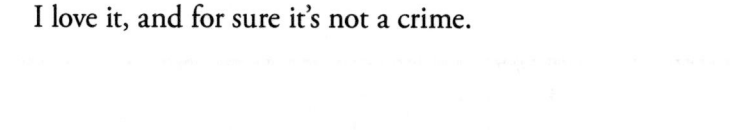

For this is my way of life at all times,
I love it, and for sure it's not a crime.

....

(16) Looking afar.

As a baby I could see but recognize not,
Becoming a child, I see, recognized and never forgot.
Growing to maturity, I see, recognized, understood and remembered,
So today in myself, I felt good, and I am not a pretender.

Looking afar, I can now see clearly,
No matter what the hours are, late or early.
My life and my future are now in sight,
So whatever I do, it will be in my right.

Out into the changing world, I have seen,
The many things seen, in which I was really keen.
I am feeling happy, content and sound,
Realizing I have seen so far all around.

To you my friends always look afar,
Admire all the bright lights, such as the stars,
That would brighten your life into a sweet tomorrow,
Light that gives joys and happiness to banish all sorrows.

....

(17) I will be home.

I will be home, home again once more,
For I never forget the fun, excitement and cares.
Of such a beautiful world outside,
But someday back to Jamaica that I cherished with pride.

I will be home to my sweet, sweet Jamaica,
This is my island of many, many acres,
To enjoy the sounds of the reggae beat,
And never to worry about the sun's heat.

I will be home again, to this lovely island,
Where happiness is like Disneyland.
Home again, from the world and its heavy strains,
Back to this beautiful island with its sunshine and rain.

I will be home again, to the sea, waves and showers,
Touching and smelling the island's fragrant flowers.
Such beauty that made Jamaica so fresh and healthy,
An island filled with love, laughter and much tranquility.

....

(18) Come Jamaica way.

There is a little island in the West Indies called Jamaica,
A place you can visit, and make your life merrier.
It's an island with lots of sunshine,
An island for sure you will find very fine.

Pack your bag, your lot and briefcase,
Or come along with only your suitcase,
To lovely Jamaica, an island in the sun,
And in every ways you will get all the fun.

Jamaica, just called it the fun side of the world,
Where joys and happiness do unfurled,
Lovely and lively music both night and days,
For sure you will never find yourself in a daze.

Come see Port Royal, Montego Bay, St. Thomas and St. Ann,
Places that you will get all the sun tan.

Great scenery in St. Mary, St. Catherine and Clarendon,
There everyone seems to have things well done.

Westmoreland, Trelawny, St. Elizabeth and Manchester,
Really lovely, and with better scenes than Westminster,
Kingston, St. Andrew and lovely Portland,
Because Portland is the place they called Pork-land.

Come see all the beauty that's there waiting,
Take pride in all of its beauty, and give it your rating,
Memories you'll never forget in Jamaica, after your visit.
Come back again, for the feelings you could never resist.

....

(19) My toiling years.

My toiling years began on the day of birth,
There I was born in a house close to a church.
From a wonderful mother with lots of love,
Lovely she was, loving and nice like an angel from above.

Boyhood days I sold snow-cones and ice cream,
It was hard work, as my body at times sent off some steam.
Many days I did some work in my father's business,
At such times, I wasn't involved in any foolishness.

Worked independently at first as an insurance agent,
But wow! Just couldn't get enough consent.
Into the civil service I strayed,
There again I found it tough both night and day.

Soon I decided after all, to fly across the isles,
But as I flew across, thousands and thousands of miles.
In England and into a factory I found a job,
Happy I was, there was no time to sob.

With low pay, hard work and in a cold weather,
I felt like a horse climbing up a ladder.
But knowing what I need, I just toiled along,
For I knew I was right, so I did not go wrong.

I worked in a bakery, a cycle shop and in transportation,
I worked also, in a milk factory, as a drum washer and a salesman.
I worked very hard, with smiles and adoration,
No matter what others say, I know I am a statesman.

I toiled the hours, the days and nights,
So the years worked, were like climbing a thousand flights.
But reminiscing on my toiling years, yes! It was great fun,
Like relaxing on the beach and enjoying the lovely sun.

Very soon to the alter I went with a lovely lady,
Although I wasn't quite prepared and really ready,
Our vow was made, as we become husband and wife,
From such moment we are still enjoying a great life.

Year by year our children came along,
And as the years went by, I watched them grew strong.
Sweet and happy years together we all enjoyed,
Yes! I am happy, I am feeling buoyed.

Whoever said life and hard work isn't beautiful,
Are only those who sit back and never tried to be dutiful,
My toiling years, could never be forgotten,
And I pray the years ahead will never be saddened.

....

(20) My beautiful hours.

The beautiful hour began at birth,
Then the hour of baptism in mother's church.

With hours and days of good wishes that followed,
Many would laugh, some smiled, and even sorrows.

Lots of youthful years of pleasures,
Others with my self enjoyed for sure.
Hours with friends as we strolled the darkness,
Feeling very happy; but sometimes we are in sadness.

The time came, and I passed the civil servant test,
It was a tough course to complete, with little hours of rest.
Hours together with friends, enjoying good food and fun,
Happily I enjoyed it, after all my hours run.

My hours in flying across the ocean,
Those moments gave me warm feelings and emotions.
Flying for hours, as I watched the clouds hid the earth,
With my open eyes, I wondered like the birds which perch.

Hours I sat in Hyde Park of London,
And admire the crowd of people, enjoying themselves at random.
Hours, with keen eyes admiring the lovely flowers,
While sitting on a bench far away from the towers.

My wedding day was filled with happiness for the ceremony,
It was a lovely day of celebration, so sweet like honey.
Lovely wedding cake, great guest and lots of champagne
There were great hours of fun, with no one being insane.

Flying again, and admiring scenes from the height,
It's a pity for those who don't have their sight.
For it is so lovely to fly out into space,
Fast, smooth, breath-taking, because it's not a race

Hours I ventured into the crowded streets,
To admire the scenes, watched the crowd and enjoy the treats.
Night time, with lights of all colors, and most of them yellow,
Some were soft, bright and nice as the sweet jello.

Those glorious hours I fully remembered,
Many times which made me feel to be kinder.
This was my life and its beautiful hours,
Hours I loved and adore, and hours that never made me sour.

....

(21) My visit to Jamaica.

Stepping onto the warm and happy Jamaican soil,
My soul felt as if I was in a boil.
Nice to be home, to all these joys and fun,
There I behold everyone enjoying the brilliant sun.

As for the nights that I was never lonely,
For within myself I was just homely.
As I heard the barking dogs, lovely music and chirping birds,
All seemed to be out there as if in a herd.

Lying in bed and listened as the rain pours,
Oh! It's so lovely, and I feel good for sure.
Where else could the raindrops sound so fine?
Right here in Jamaica, this island of mine.

Nights I watched the moon rose to its tabernacle,
 Where? In this lovely island called Jamaica.
Where the lights made the wet leaves glorious in appearance,
So lovely and touching, I wondered, should I dance?

Mornings, I watched the sun rose from the horizon,
As I relax comfortably, in my soft cushion.
The sun seems to be so different from the world I roamed,
Than the one I sat and watched at home.

Many born in this island, have now turned their backs,
To some other land, that does not hold any better stacks.

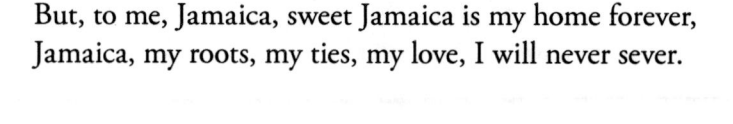

But, to me, Jamaica, sweet Jamaica is my home forever,
Jamaica, my roots, my ties, my love, I will never sever.

(22) Love.

Love is something, so wonderful and so great,
To each and everyone who have strong faith.
And to whom that love is given unto,
To be accepted and cherished as a fortune.

Love can destroy and love can conquer,
Love real love can make anyone surrender.
For true love is so good to the human body,
As it builds, strengthened and make one steady.

Real love can never be bought or sold,
In this way, it would sooner or later grow very cold.
Love that is freely given, is always better accepted,
And even for those who had been rejected.

Love can be seen in a touch, a glance or just a smile,
For true love appeared in all different styles.
Good love is the real gift of forever friendship,
That may develop into a good relationship.

(23) The loss of a loved one.

Take your time and think of the joys of today,
Remember also, that we were created from the early days.
Think of the wonders of this, our surroundings,
This great life that is so wonderful, before it's tumbling.

Life will come to an end, and all would be gone,
Actually, with the loss of a lovely loved one.
Gone, gone and maybe forever,
A loved one left us sad and sore with some kind of fever.

The feelings of unhappiness would surely grasps you,
With the loss of our loved one who was so very true.
The teardrops fall as raindrops from the sky,
As the loss and loneliness will forever make one cries.

The moment when one needed some relief,
That would uplift the feelings of one's grief.
And give one much support, strength and more faith,
That could keep us from showing to anyone, hate.

The loss of a family, a friend or a relative,
Sure, such a loss makes life feel very negative.
But we must be strong, and not to worry too much,
Though our loved ones we no longer can touch.

Now the teardrops ceased, but the memories lingered on,
But life goes on, so let us mature again and blossom,
Remembering that God made us all, so he will take us away,
So what more should we do, but trust and frequently pray.

....

(24) Dreams.

Dreams are part of all mankind,
And maybe even the animals we tend.
Dreams of tomorrows and yester-years,
That sometimes brings out of us, lots of tears.

Dreams of the world of much happiness,
Dreams that shows hate and sometimes kindness.

Dreams of the world as a battle ground,
Happy or frightened to awoke from dreams so sound.

Night dreams, day dreams and sweet dreams,
Are sometimes like those running streams,
That runs silently along the valleys deep,
As you lie there in a comfortable sleep.

Dreams that made you happy or sad,
Being awakened we are sometimes glad.
So out of such dreams and being awake,
Too bad realizing that such dreams are fakes.

Good dreams are dreams to be remembered,
Rough and ugly dreams, cause one to awake and ponder.
Good dreams should be our prayers always,
So before we go to sleep, we must always pray.

....

(25) My daughter.

In my youth I saw a movie titled the fly,
A movie that moved me and made me cried.
It was being starred by Elizabeth Taylor,
To me it was great, and she was no failure.

From then on, I admired her as the greatest actress,
Seeing her, I wondered, could she be my mistress?
So be it, for I admired and loved her quite well,
So from that day and in my heart she forever dwell.

Soon I met a woman, and from her came a lovely daughter,
She was born with love, with joys and glitter.
With Miss Taylor in my heart, I named her Elizabeth,
She is lovely, so sweet, and she is my sure bet.

Elizabeth, my daughter is a wonderful charm,
She is awesome, wonderful and very calm.
She is bright, charming and ambitious,
And with all this, she is very cautious.

She is tall, slim, neat and gracious,
A word to describe her correctly, she is just glamorous.
A daughter, a lovely girl who we loved so well,
With her charms, we have a story to tell.

Elizabeth, our daughter and sweet baby,
Whatever happens around you, we would always rally.
You are blessed, and you were destined to come our way,
God bless you, for we are sure you will never go astray.

....

(26) A loved one lost.

To lose a real and close loved one,
Somehow is discouraging even to our very bone.
It's the feelings that just ripped into one's soul,
That caused one to feel really cold.

Heartaches and head pains, may rock the body,
That caused your life to become so un-steady.
Sick within your soul, that's the kind of feelings,
Only a strong heart can stop you from screaming.

Tears flowed from the weakened eyes,
And all around everyone just cries.
For you have to be there to say goodbye,
He was our loved one and yesterday he died,

Everyone, are now in pains and sorrows,
Who can only hope for the best comes tomorrow.

Sisters, brothers, relatives, mother and father,
All together, at that moment we sadly gather.

With nieces, nephews, strangers and friends,
All would be there to attend.
The last gathering for a respectable person,
To whom we all stopped and ponder the reason.

Long would live in our hearts this terrible loss,
Of someone great to whom we all had focus.
Our lives, our aims, dreams and aspirations,
But for us all, this will also be our destination.

That sickening feelings of sorrow you never had,
Until your own experiences that made you feel sad.
That is the way for all of us,
So we must continue to hope, pray and trust.

The very bones are now weak from crying,
But the memories of a loved one, was never dying.
As the soul is now hidden deep and away,
Back to our way of life again we go, to hope and pray.

....

(27) Live right.

Live right upon this glorious land so bright,
As we all enjoy, love and maturing very well.
Just in the way we all stand upright,
As we live, tomorrow we will have something to tell.

Let wisdom, love and understanding,
Be within us each passing hour,
Just like driving on a road that is winding,
So, make others happy, as you feel under the shower.

Live good brothers, sisters and friends,
For this world will not be able to satisfy us all.
So, let's try to be very, very kind,
To the end, we will stand very tall.

This world we live in, is just like a paradise,
But you must have the cares to accept it, in this way.
Otherwise, accept and enjoy the many surprises,
That could make one speechless, with not much to say.

....

(28) Never grudge.

Never grudge, for this life is too sweet,
You could very well find yourself in deceit.
Never grudge, surely your life would be more respectable,
Like dining with friends, and enjoying lovely vegetables.

Never grudge, it's a kind of sickness to the appetite,
Think and ask yourself; is grudging really right?
Never grudge, no matter how needed and depressed you are,
Stand up, trust, pray and hope god will let you see afar.

Just never grudge, no matter what life maybe,
Work hard, keep looking up and you will see,
More pleasant and beautiful things in front of you,
Sure, lots and lots more, and not just a few.

....

(29) Ambition.

Ambition, and it's a very sweet word to sing,
So in our hearts and minds, it must always ring.

It should be the number one thought in our daily routine,
And our lives would always be fine.

This life without being ambitious,
Is like the feelings to yourself of being suspicious.
Ambition will elevate you to the top of success,
So don't be in fear, it's not like a drug test.

Fear not, just be ambitious,
Ambition breeds success, as prayer makes you religious.
Ambition will forward a decent and upright life,
In which you would always find delight.

Do not take the idea of ambitiousness for granted,
Deep within you it should always be implanted,
In order to attain the heights of honor,
Like the joys and happiness of the athlete runner.

Let our lives be surrounded in ambitiousness,
Like those who keep their hearts in tenderness.
Let it be our only goal, ambition and aspiration,
That in the future, we will be happy to stand at attention.

....

(30) Tomorrow.

Tomorrow will be another day for me,
Sure, another day for me to love, enjoy and see.
What will tomorrow be for me and for you?
Let's hope it will bring all our wishes true.

Life today is really beautiful and so great,
Yet tomorrow we maybe in for a real sweat.
But, let's not worry too much about tomorrow,
Only pray and hope there will be no sorrows.

This is a world filled with tomorrow's joys,
Sweet and happy, just like the little girls and boys.
So never worry about what maybe in store,
Let's all enjoy today, and tomorrow hope for more.

Tomorrow could be the day of some kind of decision,
It could be for progress, unity or division.
So let's accept the sweet moments of today,
And pray that tomorrow we will see more of the sun.

....

(31) Hyde Park. (Speaker's corner, London England.)

Speaker's corner, it's in the heart of London,
A park that is always up to date, and never run down.
A lovely place to be, speaker's corner or Hyde Park,
Where on al Sundays, one will find lots of sparks.

Ethnic groups from all other countries,
Speaking their words, like doctors prescribing remedies.
The people speak all they wished to say,
Some sing, dance, play, talk or play.

Many speakers on makeshift podiums of any kind,
They send out their messages with tongue and signs.
From their podium that maybe a stool or chair,
But looking closely, many podiums are really rare.

Some speakers perched on benches, ladders or tables,
They worked from anything in which they were able.
Everyone doing their thing and saying their words,
Speaking loud, so everyone could come forward.

Beautiful Hyde Park, packed with wonderful people,
The young, middle aged, the elderly and feeble,

All are there to share and enjoy the fun,
With comments, criticism, friendliness as they enjoy the sun.

....

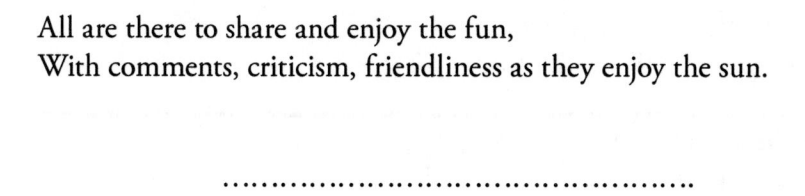

(32) Spring time.

It's spring time in lovely Canada once more,
The ice, the slush and the cold are all gone,
And now the beauty of nature's best can be seen,
To each and everyone who are really keen.

Springtime and the flowers are coming out,
The leafless trees are again filled with spouts,
The tulips, brightens in their glorious colors and mixtures,
And only time will show that some are tortured.

Springtime and everyone seemed to start afresh,
Its spring, its cleaning time, let's pick up the trash,
The young, the middle aged and the elderly,
Each and everyone cherished this time so dearly.

Canada's spring and all around are filled with happiness,
Sometimes there is sadness, but for sure, there is kindness.
Shared by all the people, birds and animals,
That springs forth daily as the year's perennials.

....

(33) Young Street. (Toronto)

Toronto, Yonge street, oh! It is so beautiful,
On this street everyone tried to be dutiful.
Yonge Street, is a street that divides the whole city,
A very long street that is really pretty.

No they named it Yonge Street,
And all along the street, it's smiles with lots of treats.

This is the longest street in the world,
With actually all stores decorated with many pearls.
Yonge Street for sure, provides a lot of happiness,
Will all its beauty and natural softness.

Yonge Street has got all the touch of tenderness,
There at all times glorified with love and kindness.
Most of the people are always in a happy mood,
As they enjoy themselves with lots of good food.

Admire the lovely ladies in their mini skirts,
In spring, fall, summer and even winter, that makes one flirts.
Gazed into the beauty of the well fashioned windows,
So lovely they are, filled with delight as playing bingos.

People from all different races and nations,
Are there to see, enjoy and shop for bargains.
The lights of the nights are a delight,
Because those lights, are all designed so right.

Everyone should really see the charms of Yonge,
It could even jolt you and make you young.
Remember if you need peace of mind,
Just come to Yonge Street, and you will find,
Your heart's desires happiness and fulfillment.
Yonge Street, come along, for your comments or torment.

....

(34) How Lucky.

Sure, today is my day of real good luck,
For I have met someone, sweet and lovely.

To you my dear I will be forever stuck,
Our love and cares will very friendly.

How lucky, in meeting such a wonderful woman,
So sweet, charming, and full of caring.
That's why your remembrance will always remain,
With all the love we need to sustain.

That was the lucky day our stars appeared,
With blessings, the glory of love came to us.
Showing us what we were about to share,
It was real love, true love with respect and trust.

This moment sweetheart is our lucky day,
Though we did not talk about our friendship,
It was love in our hearts, with not much to say,
But in our hearts, we were ready for a relationship.

So we grow forward from this day on,
As we look forward to walk hand in hand.
Let's pray that God will guide our path,
As we ponder and share our thoughts.

....

(35) Summertime.

It's summer time in beautiful Toronto,
When most people head to a place called harbor front,
Many pack their backs with towels called pronto,
For sightseeing, digest fast foods, and wipe away the junks.

Summertime is here for all, once more,
So everyone, are very happy for sure,
The beautiful and soft flowers all filled our taste,
And all around there is little land at waste.

The parks are glorious, clean, beautiful to bring the people in,
So come visit them, for there are lots to make you grin,
It's the time of the year when everyone watered the gardens,
And banish away all the bugs and rodents.

Summertime, so wonderful when it's here,
Only that it just won't last for a year.
Fun, pleasure, excitement and happiness,
And for sure everyone is doing some tidiness.

Summer time and everyone are so joyous,
And all around everything is really gorgeous.
This is the season for the joggers and cyclists,
They all moved swiftly and with a twist.

Summertime is beautiful in Toronto, and it's just great!
With people who tried to get into some sweat,
Nice to admire the boaters on the lake in the hundreds,
With everyone so organized and in good friendship.

....

(36) Our love affair.

Our love affair is one to be cherished,
With all our wishes, that should never vanish.
Memories of our love affair we would always remember,
Soon our love will grow, and we become real tender.

Thoughts of you are real joys to my life,
Sure we will be together without any strife.
That would be memories to our forever love affair,
As we showed each other our real tender cares.

Our love affair is like the doctor's medicine,
That is administered to cure our ills, leaving no signs.

A medicine of love, that cures us of all our problems,
And our contentment will be lovely as an emblem.

Our love affair forever, will last and last,
Sure we would never be seen like an outcast.
So let's cherish our love affair forever,
And with experiences, we should be very clever.

Our love affair will be blessed forever,
With God's help, we will not severe our love.
Our love affair will grow in strength,
So strong, that tomorrow, it will never be bent.

....

(37) Winter season...... (Canada)

Canada's winter days are here,
It's a time to be inside, to look out and stare.
Looking and wondering on the outside cloudiness,
And at times gave the one feeling of loneliness.

Sometimes many got into their car for a winter's ride,
Far and wide out into the countryside,
Where one admired the hills and valleys bare,
Without any worries heartaches or fears.

The leaves are almost gone,
And the icicles are about to be born.
Up and around, with a few birds flying around,
Only for them there is not much food to be found.

Winter is so beautiful in many ways,
Joys to the skaters in the parks, slopes and alleyways,
Sighting of icicles hanging from trees and houses,
With nearly everyone dressed in trousers.

To enjoy Canada's beautiful shades of winter,
Does uplift your spirit as watching a great sprinter,
The weather doth changed in different ways,
Just the way you would walk through a maze.

Not many smiles in winter time,
Although many would say it's just fine.
Outside there may be lots of snow and slippery ice,
While inside most watch T.V., gossip and enjoy some cooked rice,

Winter so beautiful with its white soft snow,
So, lovely as the little girl's head bow.
What better joys as Canada's winter memories,
This is fascinating as the sweet and lovely bunnies.

....

(38) Open your heart.

Let's open our hearts to all around,
Human, animals, insects, birds and even trees,
For that is where wonderful love is found,
And for sure our hearts would always be free.

Open our hands and hearts to all,
The rich, the poor, the sick or frail,
And with that openness come God's blessings,
That is far better than trespassing.

Open your hearts and ears to the needy,
While reminiscing on those that are greedy,
With love and a tender loving heart,
So far from you, no one would ever depart.

An open heart would give love to the world,
With beauty as lovely as our curls,

That always shines in the eyes of admirers,
Giving satisfaction to everyone's desires.

Open your heart to everyone it is a great blessing,
Open your heart, its so interesting.
An open heart means blessings from above
It's the blessings from God with all his love.

....

(39) Dark night in Toronto. (In Toronto.)

  This short poem was written after the big blackout in Toronto, Ontario on Wednesday night April 25th. 1990. I tried to call the radio station that was covering the night's episode, CFRB, but they were so busy, I just couldn't get through, so soon after I decided to put my knowledge of that night into this short poem.
  Wednesday April 25th. Nineteen-hundred and ninety, a black out that gave a lot of people a real fright, as it was dark over here, but over yonder there was plenty of light.

Driving along quietly on Eglington Ave west,
A warm evening, so lots of people were out in their vests,
Everything seemed to be beautiful and calm,
The lights, the houses, people and trees were just a charm.

Which was first, it's hard to tell,
A sudden flash of light toward the sky,
And all around instant darkness fell,
The lights were gone, it was dark and I felt some what shy.

Yes! There was a ball of fire going to the clouds,
It was something to worry, nothing to be proud.
What is this, I stopped and wondered,
Was it lightening, thunder or a bomb from yonder?

At this moment the world seemed silent,
With whistling sirens all in the urgent,
My eyes hath seen a while ago,
And suddenly it's dark like a fast blow.

My eyes did saw light, but now I was in darkness,
My own ears heard the explosion, as I sense the darkness,
And I cannot forget that station CFRB,
That carried the dilemma around and abroad.

Home I hustled to find my home alight,
With everyone very happy and just bright,
So I switched again to CFRB radio station,
Just to listen to more news coming from the nation.

I tried to contact them another a half a dozen times,
But I found it easier to count a thousand dimes,
So I sat back in my cozy chair to get the facts,
Because it was impossible to do so by fax.

To listened the experiences of the dilemma of the people,
Their words somehow made me tremble.
The blue jays were playing, so the fans did not hear,
Good it was, maybe there would be a rush out, in fear.

....

(40) Martin Luther King.

He was a man born of black parentage,
Grown in maturity and sometimes bondage,
He loved each and everyone, without a spot of malice,
Because Dr. King was not born in a palace.

They called him Martin Luther King junior,
No one so good before, had ever come sooner,

Without pride or malice he spoke for us all,
In history he is remembered in the winter, spring summer and fall.

He was born a true, honest and faithful black American,
So he was known and heard by the nations,
Martin we will again see you in person for sure,
So your words and works are in our hearts forevermore.

Dr. King, a man who toiled for years and years,
Preaching human rights for all to hear,
Never afraid of a fight or the gun,
That's why upon him always shine the sun.

He fought with words for the rights of human dignity,
In every town, in every city and vicinity,
He was one of America's best eloquent speakers,
a Baptist minister, whom the world respected as a true leader.

....

(41) Wars.

Wars should be classified as infinity,
It's fought to destroy the human dignity.
Brought about by the greed of someone,
Whom one could only called troublesome.

What good are wars to the human race?
Tragic they are, as they destroy the human face.
In the east, the west, the south and the north,
There is no place a war was never been fought.

Arms race and wars are degrading,
When the world is hungry and need upgrading,
Leaders of this lovely world, adopt yourself to some realization,
And stop now the arms race and mobilization.

The world hungry needed food for their strength,
Not wars that only give us a stench,
By taking away our loved ones forever,
Who with a true heart could say that's very cleaver?

It's time to put all wars behind us,
Forever, no one or no part of the world will fuss,
So that we all can live together to the end,
And to the throne, our God would help us to ascend.

....

(42) Work.

To work is one's greatest way to exercise,
For only those who are willing and ready to decide.
Work is very good for each and everyone,
The rich, the poor, the happy and the lonesome.

Let's enjoy every minute of the work we do,
As it helps us to wear a good pair of shoes,
Life may be dull without a day working,
Or it may be listless as the animals in need of feeding.

Every minute of work is a blessing to life,
Although at times you find yourself in strife,
But that is the way to life's success,
And that's the way our eyes should all focus.

Work and lots of work put the mind at ease,
So from our minds bad thoughts would erase,
For that is what work is all about,
To build you up and cast away all doubts.

Work is to work at all types of jobs,
No matter the quality clothes in which you clad,

Whatever job one does, free or for wages,
One's life will be turned like a book with interesting pages.

Ambition will inspire any one do any work,
Un-ambitiousness enables one to sit and lurk,
Any work, every job will help to make one busy,
But remember there is no work that is very easy.

Never sit around and wait for something,
Always get out and do some hunting,
Find some work no matter what it maybe,
For sure you will have a brighter future to see,

No lazy person can survive for very long,
When daily they just sit around humming a song,
Not realizing that their life is on a downward trend,
To which only luck can help them to ascend.

....

(43) My wedding knot.

This day has a very special hour for two wonderful people,
Who has not seen their decision as feeble,
We both have planned a life so sweet in taste,
not knowing what in tomorrow we may face.

She as my bride, walks and sat with such fulgency,
And the groom was very bright and efficient.
Cameras flashing and smiling friends all looked glorious,
All have made this day and hour just gracious.

In our ears the wind whispers sweet melodious tunes,
As we became husband and wife this afternoon,
Reminiscing on the love words that always chimes,
And this day they come to roost with patience and time.

God bless our marriage and togetherness,
As we live the years ahead with progress,
Prosperity, and long life in God's Holy name,
For sure we would never be ashamed.

....

(44) Debt.

In this beautiful life, nearly everyone has got some debts,
But after this beautiful life, there comes death.
We borrow, so therefore we owe every single day,
Sure, we indebted ourselves far more than we pray.

Debts are created because of our everyday needs,
But it is created by some, all because of greed.
The poorer we are, it's more trouble whenever we borrow,
Then sometimes we may find ourselves in sorrow.

Creating a debt is almost everyone's game,
But to many of us it's like a real shame.
But no matter what one does these days,
Debt, like the sunshine brings to you some rays.

The nations of the world, all have a debt problem.
Like the flag they fly as an emblem.
Countries and people borrow to upgrade their standards of living,
And with all this they joined hands to do some giving.

Creating debts is sometimes an everlasting pain,
But we all needed it, as we needed the rain.
And although it puts a drain in our [pockets,
It does help a lot to fill their closets.

By creating debts, we cam also create a burden on our souls,
Where we wonder, and sigh, if it's a real mole.

But just remember, we may not be able to start anew,
But the only person to blame is you.

....

(45) Drugs.

Try and never let your heart be addicted,
Sooner or later your body could be affected.
Drugs do cause sweats and bad curses,
And sometimes leave you with lots of bruises.

Forget drugs, never look for it, forget it, and never look back,
Go in search of something new, try the athletic track.
Run, walk, confer, read, or watch the others in some fun,
That would be better than looking back to a gun.

When you are afflicted or addicted to drugs,
It's like having on your body a million bugs.
If drugs is in your sight, turn yourself away,
never allowed your heart and mind to be swayed.

Let us all keep the air fresh and clean,
Fresh, lovely and clean, just like the sweet beans.
Drug addicts, don't allow yourself to be the one, singled out,
You would be the one with all the doubts.

Let drugs be only a dreamy memory,
Better things are there in glory.
Forget it, leave it and disregard it,
You will be happy and the world will be fit.

....

(46) Taxis.

In every [part of this world there are taxis,
They could be number one in a real crisis.
They moved everyone fast to their destinations,
in the nights or days, sunshine or rain to the physician.

The quality of service is always great,
And a service no one could ever hate.
Get in, sit comfortably and ride along,
Comfortably as the baby lie in the prom,

Taxis are of different colors and makes,
So it doesn't matter which one you take,
Phone them, or even flag them down,
They are ready to take you on your round.

Taxis are an important service to every one,
Riding in two's, three's, four's are alone.
They could be at your service always,
Whether going near or far away.

....

(47) Politicians.

Politicians to me are like comedians,
They are cloaked in political fakes upon their podiums.
Friendly, with promises before any election,
But being elected, they all forget their decisions.

Promises to the people, that maybe only God could do,
Elected to office they become very crude or rude.
Con men are all politicians, this we all should know,
They begged with tears for vote, to inherit their dough.

One could called them just haughty,
Many elected politicians or downright naughty.
In the way they stooped to be elected,
Then elected you, your x, and your needs are neglected.

Never I say ever trust any politician,
It's better to put your trust in a magician.
Nor magicians would trick you, and that you realize,
To me politicians only sucks one, until one is paralyze.

This is your right, they preach, so came, vote for me,
But it's only a pity many cannot see.
The hunger in them to enjoy tax payer's money,
All in store and ready to drink like sweet honey.

For that is the way they make fast buck,
Fast and quick from the tax payer's back.
In order to ride high in the years of glory,
Psychologically saying aloud, they are working for the poorly.

....

(48) Canada.

Years ago I heard the names of countries far and strange,
Thinking of them all seemed to be out of range.
Finally I decided to leave my country for another,
By choice I decided and choose Canada.

This Canada, a country filled with virtues and knowledge,
No wonder it has got so many colleges.
For the real ambitious, it's a lovely place to be,
And there are lots to enjoy, see and read.

Canada, oh yes! Such a beautiful country,
It's people, with great ideas for another century.

Come see the office towers rising over the hills,
Faster than how you could raise your bills.

People of all class and from all nations,
Are here in Canada enjoying the outdoors, indoors or in a congregation.
All Canadians are lovely people, warm and filled with adorations,
No wonder we are so proud to be Canadians.

It was my own choice to be a Canadian,
I made Canada my home, and that's my decision.
No matter who wish to complain or want to cry,
To lovely and beautiful Canada I won't say goodbye.

Buildings are vast, lovely and terribly in heights,
At nights when the lights are lit, they are really bright.
And the beauty of the designs are even better seen,
Even if someone's eyes are not too keen.

In Canada, there is always a sense of humor with each other,
Which seems to make everyone looks much better.
The climate and the touch of happiness all around,
Oh! To all my friends, this Canada will make you feel sound.

There may be small problems here and there,
But what clothes one wear that will not tear.
So see Canada, love and enjoy Canada with all its qualities,
It is well blessed with all its charities.

....

(49) Beggars.

The beggars, who for sure could have done passed work,
But today they ponder, they wonder and they lurk.
In the alley ways, the valleys and on the side walks,
And to themselves, one would constantly hear them talk.

Dirty they may appear in shabby clothes and hair,
So many people would ignore them, out of fear.
But although they may never hurt anyone,
Their appearance at times seemed real troublesome.

Beggars would put out their shaking hands,
To anyone, just hoping someone would be kind.
Many would offer them whatever they could find,
But a few un-kindly ones would ignore and wined.

Give them a dime, a nickel or a penny,
Because they may not need a lot of money,
For some would only spend it on cheap wines,
Being satisfied with their way of life to be just fine.

You may stop and watch the beggars doing their chores,
That could riddle your soul like an inside soar.
Deep in poverty and treated with disdain,
Are like those in disgrace and filled with aching pains.

....

(50) The brave.

Let's be brave and face up to all realities,
That our lives could adopt with all responsibilities.
Be brave in whatever you think of doing,
As bravery should be the goal of all human beings.

Be brave, and ambition would easily be accomplished,
That is something any one would be proud to cherish.
Like a soldier, strong, brave, and without fear,
For with such braveness, one may not care.

Be brave so that there are no fears in order to succeed,
In any wish, all tasks, desires and deeds.

The world today should be brave and fearless,
Although there are many who do not care less

The people in this world should be always brave,
Showing authority with all the things we face,
So, let's be brave and try to change the world,
In a way no one could ever unfold.

....

(51) The alphabet.

The alphabet consisted of only twenty six letters,
They were put together just like feathers.
I could write the letters all to you,
And that you would find so very true.

Twenty six letters and a trillion words,
And still I could always strive and move forward.
With interest in writing that made me felt real strong,
I don't think I could ever be bored or go wrong.

Read those words and letters, again and again,
To your life and your progress there won't be any strain,
For those letters could point out what's in you and me,
And that would be there for all to see.

The alphabet can be so easily jumbled,
Very easy and not very hard like getting a tumble,
The alphabet is the first phase of learning,
For that is where our lives began its turning.

....

(52) The gambler.

With a pocket of money, head with ideas, he is off to do his thing,
It's the gambler on the prowl going to his fling.
It doesn't matter if he wins or if he loses,
It's his decision, so he does whatever he pleases.

Bet one, bet two, three or even a dozen,
Until his mind, body and soul is frozen.
Into something that continue to needle him,
Although he would never think it's really a sin.

He does what he loves and what he enjoys,
Just like playing with the girls and boys.
Without fears or doubts, but with confidence and a little carefree,
With one or the other, for him it's just a spree.

Glory days would take him home in happiness,
Tough luck, unlucky days may drive him into madness,
But that is the life the gambler cherished,
And he always hoped that one day he would be rich.

....

(53) Prejudice or racism.

The Almighty God made us all, if you believe,
Hope you do for your soul would be relieved.
He created the world, animals, insects, trees, creatures, you and me,
He gave all, eyes so that we can all see.

We are here together as a family,
So no one should ever be treated with notoriety.
Accept each other with dignity and not with disdain,
Respect and love in this life we would all retain.

Never look at another person to be different,
Because people are not like vehicles you rent.
The only difference is the colors of people's skin,
Seen only by some people whose hearts are filled with racism.

Understand, that below the skin is the same human touch,
Light a candle, turn a bulb or light a torch,
For whatever is there, being a racist would always be seen'
So in yourself, be understanding and have nothing to fear.

Remember in this world there are many racist people,
Within them, their hearts and minds are just like a weevil.
Again be yourself, think wisely or join a group,
Speak no evil, see no evil, join the company and enjoy some soup.

Oh! You ignorant and racist people of the world,
Come forward with love and let it be told,
That the signs of prejudice and racism are both gone afoul,
And never again you would be called a fool.

Love blossoms in the hearts of those that see no prejudice,
That would make one lifestyle more clean and religious.
And would allow us to live together in love and happiness,
Banishing racism, all bitterness as we stopped prejudice.

....

(54) The cyclist.

Here they come in twos four and more, the cyclists,
They moved very fast, all doing some kind of a twist.
On their bicycles after a quick and fast mount,
They rode swiftly up the hill and around the mound.

Onto the streets they made their way,
With tight grips, full balance and little to say,

Moving fast, some with smiles, others serious and cool,
Observing everything and sometimes obeying all the rules.

Bobbling, weaving around people and over bumps,
Almost looking like warriors ready to pounce,
True, they made some problems for others to worry,
With only a few stop to say i am sorry.

Moving at times dangerously and risky,
Wow! Sometimes they made a lot of people go tipsy,
Good luck to them, just pray they safely returned,
Free from all accidents and with out any burns.

Let it be safe wherever you ride,
Alone, in company or even beside,
A good cyclist can make a lot of people happy,
And would never make anyone felt very sloppy.

....

(55) Never disregard.

God made us all, so together we should enjoy a good life,
Upon this land, together in happiness and without any strife,
To make a better world for our future generation,
And without any disregard for anyone in this nation.

Never disregard the young or helpless,
You could find your mind become very restless.
Never disregard the feeble or the poor,
That could cause your heart and soul to become sour.

Never disregard the animal, birds or insects,
They too, could also be of good friendship,
Never disregard the sufferings of anyone in a plight.
And those who never or will ever get their rights.

Finally never disregard love and tenderness,
Even for those who are down and in distress.
And never, never disregard god the almighty,
he is the only one who will judge us correctly.

....

(56) Aim high.

Keep your head high and with an aim,
In the years ahead you will never be the same,
Keep your head up and your spirit high,
As others may lose theirs with only a sigh.

Aim high and with ambitious thoughts,
Never be dull that could put you in a wrath,
Aim high with strength to hold firm,
There will be benefits and happiness in later years to come.

Aim high, for the world owes everyman a living,
If you keep a low profile, you could find nothing.
Aim high and model yourself in every ways,
So that contentment would glorify your days.

Aim high and correctly, for this world cannot be altered for you,
In order to ascend to the path of glory you may choose,
Never try to be great by only artificial means,
For your aim and heights to reach success must be seen as clean.

Hope and aim high for all things, then patiently wait
Patiently as the fisherman with a line and his bait,
If success or your hopes, reached or not,
Would still free your mind of negligence and gives you comfort.

Aim high even if the world is not in favor of your success,
 The height to reach at times, is sometimes just a guess,

The heights to reach at times is always hard to ascend,
So just never sit idly by and only pretend.

Aim high, although there may be impossible barriers
To achieve success and sealed your future career,
Aim high, and above all discouragements,
to find joys, hopes, happiness and encouragements.

....

(57) Unity.

Unity, such a beautiful word to keep reciting,
And sometimes it made things really exciting.
So let's all unite, and let it be a way of life,
For that could help us all to survive.

Say the word, understanding fully it's meaning,
And even if you had to do it, screaming.
Unity could be a magic word in many ways,
For, with the knowledge of unity we should all crave.

A unified world, so nice to realize,
Just like going far and wide for some exercise,
Unity, so nice and such a good thing,
Let's try it, like a song, we all can sing.

Let's all unite and see the world so lucid,
Being in unity we could see ourselves like cupids,
Accepting others like sisters, brothers or friends,
Together and forever we could continue the trend.

With outstretched arms to those who are far,
Invite them in, do not only stand and stare,
A unified feeling of love, given to them all,
Would surely let them feel all tall.

So let us unite brothers and sisters,
So that we may not feel somewhat sinister,
Let's try and make a better world for all of us,
To love, sleep, eat, play, live, pray and trust.

....

(58) Jealousy.

Jealousy is like the sting of a bee to human life,
Jealousy placed many of us in a lot of strife.
From the animal, the birds and insects,
And to each and everyone it has got some effects.

Jealousy is sometimes caused from a bungled mind,
So effective it even placed many of us in a grind.
Many people does bring jealousy to themselves,
And along the way they may pray to have it dissolves.

Jealousy may arise from a thoughts or a scene,
Or from things heard, that could be, or never had been,
Restrain yourself where difficulties are concerned,
And hopefully one would never feel any disdain.

Jealousy for something or for someone,
Could bring happiness or even make one lonesome,
And sometimes create in one some feelings of strength,
So let jealousy fades away, before it tossed you to the trench.

Jealousy also helped many to attain great heights,
But it is those who worked hard or had it in sight.
Jealousy arise also, because of a lost lover,
Be calm and sensitive and just get under the covers.

Jealousy can uplift many to their aims,
But others it just degrades and sometimes maim,

So be wise and understanding in respect of jealousy,
And through this life show better courtesy.

....

(59) Let's not fear.

Let's not fear the world,
Fear can be overcome as easy as losing a curl.
Let's not fear the dread of nights,
For no ghost can ever appear in sight.

Fear not the mountain so high,
To the top you'd reach if you patiently try.
Fear not the bumps in your plight,
Hold your head high, and hold very tight.

Never fear the books of many words,
Read and retain them, for contents, could be sharp as a sword.
Never be in fear to take encouraging chances,
You must do so, in the very way you do with your glances.

Year god in this life, and never be this way or that way,
But only if you find the time to pray,
Never be saddened because of fear of resentment,
Maybe that would be the hour, comes all the sentiments.

....

(60) I wish.

I wish, I wish I was really great,
I would for sure give lots of treats,
I wish I could walk the world to promote love,
For I love to be on the move.

I wish I had a lot more brains,
Then there would be little less strain,
For I would train and educate all, for a happier world,
And lovely people in my arms a lot more to enfold.

I wish I could turn the world around,
Maybe, I would make everyone wear a crown.
And live to enjoy a life of sweet tomorrows,
In this lovely world, and be free from sorrows.

I wish I could bring unity to all mankind,
And let everyone put all the bad tastes behind.
Oh! What a world I wish I could have,
This world with wishes and no one would starve.

....

(61) Seven negatives of life.

Today's pathway of life has given many of us **fear**,
Because, the path to success is never really clear.
Some only accumulate within themselves **jealousy**,
But it's better to think of things more righteously.
Never filled your heart and mind with **hatred**,
It should always be clear and sacred.
Never in your life think of being **revengeful**,
Life is much better when you live it more beautiful.
To cheat, steal, or lust for more are just **greed**,
Progress, and grow independently as the sewn seeds.
Never accept all that is said to be **suspicious**,
As that to your thinking is not too delicious.
If you failed to accomplish your ambition, never develop **anger**,
Pray, hope, trust and thank God you are still alive to lick your fingers.
With **fear, jealousy, hatred, revenge, greed, superstition and anger**,
Be very careful, they could make you be like a mourner.

So, these my readers are the seven negatives of life,
Let them be far from your thoughts, so there will be no strife.

....

(62) Night out.

Sweet are the days and lovely are the nights,
I do enjoy them within my rights.
As I stroll the quiet streets with spirit bright,
I gazed at strange objects without any fright.

I see the lovely lights flickering everywhere,
Just as lovely and beautiful as the tableware.
Nights and the moonlight is soft and touching,
The glittering stars twinkles, yet far from reacting.

Often times I wondered to a club or night spot,
I made myself comfortably as a baby in a cot.
I may drink one, two or three beers,
Some of which the tastes are so rare.

I sometimes sit, stand around or dance to the sweet music,
Standing around, admiring the lovely ladies looking so chic.
All well dressed and dancing in their lovely attires,
So glamorous they all made me felt so desired.

Night life and the tired and weary are gone to rest,
And all the birds has taken to their nests,
Night out, and seeing the young and exciting having their pleasures,
Night out to me is happiness, excitement and real treasures.

....

(63) My song. (wishes of life")

I wish I was a magician,
I would put a curse on all politicians,
I wish I had a million and more,
I would be called a millionaire.
I wish I could have a house,
Then I would roam it like a mouse.
I wish I really had lots of money,
Each day I would be only drinking honey.
I wish I had a profession,
Then I would make lots of decisions.
I wish everyone were nice and friendly,
Then we would for sure treat others kindly.
I wish I could buy everything I need,
Then I could sit back, relax, write and read.
I wish that I had wings that I could fly,
To fly the world I would really try.
I wish we all could really love one another,
Just the way all the birds flocked together.
I wish the world could be free from poverty,
So that everyone would stop giving charity.
I wish everyone could be very happy and free,
Like the lovely breeze and trees.
I wish there was no dangers in our lives,
Then we could walk all corners, valleys and sites.
I wish there was no wars of the nations,
Oh! We could breathe such sweet sensations.
I wish there could be no fighting around,
So that life could stop falling to the ground.
I wish it was possible for me to be born again,
I would for sure try to be ordained.
I wish, never to have any sins,
In the way many clothes are free from pins.
I wish I could be a Christian,
That would mean more to me than a trillion.
I wish and pray God will bless me forever,
My trust in him I would never severe.
Finally, I wish I could live forevermore,

To see, enjoy, love, cherish and adore.
I wish I could really, really sing,
My songs would make all ears continuously ring.
Bless me Lord I need it for sure,
As I promised that I would be forever pure.

....

(64) My early walk.

The night before it was bright and warm,
And the wind all around was some what calm,
Early morn and the world seemed lonely,
But my walk was just fun and leisurely.

I glanced at the twinkling lights far and wide,
As I walked briskly with no one by my side,
Joggers jogged by in strides, but not in a race,
As their directions and movements my eyes would trace.

The leaves are wet from the overnight dew,
Glistening in the wafting leaves as if they were saying adieu,
I walked many kilometers and now filled with sweat,
But I never stop to think, worry or fret.

Early walks at times I stopped and gazed,
At the lovely flowers all around and in a maze,
I hear the dogs barking and watched the cats sprint by,
I sigh and I wondered of such beauty when I looked at the sky.

....

(65) Loneliness.

Loneliness is like a single flying bee,
Loneliness like the only ant that crawls upon a tree,

Loneliness like walking alone in the dark of night,
Loneliness needed strength and stamina to fight.

Loneliness maybe an experience to all,
Tough at times, that is just like a hard fall.
Experienced by you, the animals and birds,
As we stroll, they fly and we used the roads.

Loneliness with its aches, sometimes made one sick,
And at times it placed your soul in a risk.
Sitting, sleeping or walking by one's self,
It's lonely and desperate, as the appearance of an empty shelf.

God made everyone and everything to have a companion,
Don't be lonely seek someone out, be a real champion.
Let loneliness be a thing of the past,
And never allow yourself to be an outcast.

Walking alone, gazing at the lonely sitting on a bench,
The lonely, a little rugged, with both fists clenched,
Loneliness, with outstretched hands begging for a dime,
From your pocket you hand him a few coins, he felt just fine.

Places of loneliness, the cemetery, morgue and the hospitals,
Places that give you the feelings as just being fatal,
Never must anyone disregard the lonely,
They too need to feel themselves somewhat homely.

God created us, so we should all seek happiness,
So let's try never to be somewhat worthless.
Help the lonely to be happy upon this wonderful earth,
Just like the way we find happiness when we flirt.

....

(66) Where will I turn?

Where should I turn when my eyes are open?
And as the pain and anguish both deepen.
Where will I turn when help needed, is no more?
And all such desperations make me real sore.

Where will I turn when all my friends are gone?
And with no one around to adorn,
Where will I turn when the night's lights are lit?
There is no one around and no where to sit.

Where will I turn when the sun shines?
Only in some way I may be feeling fine,
Where will I turn for love and comfort?
My love is gone, with no other coming forth.

Where will I turn when I am down and feeling depressed?
No one, or no where to make me refreshed,
And where will I turn, now that I am fallen,
I will turn to God who will do all from heaven.

....

(67) Let's not forget.

Let's not forget our wonderful parents,
They were with us every where we went.
Let's not forget our place of birth,
It could be from a palace or from the dirt.

Let's not forget our country of birth, it's our roots,
Our land filled with love from where we sprout.
Let's not forget our school friends,
And remember those we also defend.

Let's not forget our sisters and brothers,
Recalling the times we were together without any bother.
Let's not forget the things we usually do and say,
While we were together at all times, night or day.

Let's not forget the gifts and kindness,
Given or rendered so often with tenderness,
Let's not forget the flourishing times or the rough times of life,
We are still here and floating like a kite.

Let's not forget all our true friends,
They were great, they were true and they were kind,
Let's not forget life's struggles to survive,
God will bless all to come out al-right and alive.

Let's not forget our wonderful lord and savior,
As we pray today, tomorrow and forever.
Let's not forget that without god we would never be here,
So let's serve him well and have nothing to fear.

....

(68) Women.

Women, created from the rib of a man we learnt,
But they were never created only to be servants.
But to be a mother and beloved partner in life,
And for sure they were not here to pick a fight.

Life with any woman, who is dear and precious,
See them dressed, oh! They are so gracious,
A woman so good, so wonderful and so witty,
Just the way she is always nice and pretty.

She maybe a wife, a mother, a sweetheart or a dear,
A woman, obedient and willing to show lots of cares,

These wonderful women, a friend, a mother or daughter,
Who stands with a man, a companion, a father or a brother?

A woman well dressed is filled with class,
Glistening just like a shining glass,
Tempting at times to the human desires,
Admiring a woman could set one's soul on fire.

Let's be proud of who she is, a wife, a mother or a daughter,
They are women, and lots of them are teachers,
Who can render great moments of true comfort?
From which we can never depart.

So let's love and cherish all women,
They are created just like all men,
To have and enjoy a life of love and understanding,
And never do so as if one is pretending.

Who should live without a woman as our companion?
For with her, one just felt like a champion,
In all the ways she makes you feel good and wonderful,
 a wonderful woman she is, who is more than helpful.

A man should never live without a woman,
It would be very hard to feel yourself as human,
For being a lovely woman, a daughter or a wife,
They would never try to cause any strife.

....

A poem to my girlfriend and wife to be.

(69) The day I met you.

I remember that lovely day we met,
On that day it rained so we got wet.

The morning sun had just arrived,
And the world seemed awake, yes! It came alive.

I remember the wonderful smile you showed me,
I knew it meant love as far as I could see,
Your looks was an excitement to my soul,
I sigh, it was excitement, it made my thoughts rolled.

Standing speechless, my heart said, I need you,
Soon after you became my one and only beau,
We are now together from that day onward,
And nothing would stop us from going forward.

Oh it was a great day to be in that direction,
Where I met a wonderful lover, without any objection,
I felt very bright as the sun made the day,
So in the future, I would have lots more to say.

Bravely and nervously I said the words in mind,
Hello beautiful, you are the gold I wish to find,
Returning my greetings softly and tenderly,
That's all was needed to make us friendly.

Exchanging words cautiously with each other,
With the feelings and thoughts of being closer,
Shaking hands with smiles, as we said each other's name,
And sure we were happy, for the names were not the same.

Here is my number and name for you to keep,
Please keep them safely and never let me weep,
My life and happiness are now in your hands,
As the day we would stroll together on the sands.

Soon we kissed nervously, and sweetly, then good-bye,
As we both turned our back and sigh.
That was one of my greatest moments,
As I headed home to relax, sit and lament,

It was a beautiful day, and I was happy to be there,
Then I prayed that tomorrow's excitement would be forever,
I felt confident that I would never again worry or fret,
For God brought us together on that special day we met.

....

(A poem dedicated to my wife.)

(70) A lover

A lover in you today I have found,
You! Tomorrow, I pledge that you, I would never disown,
Your fingers has got such a warm touch,
So! soft and satisfying as laying on the coach.

To me the world hath seemed worthless,
Or was I lacking some kind of boldness,
To find someone as you are, a real true lover,
Who gave me warmth just like my covers?

The smiles from your lovely awesome face,
Your body so sexy, and tempting for a warm embrace,
You are a lover, really true and filled with life,
A book about you, I would someday write.

Your mind is wondering and your eyes filled with love,
I wondered if you had just descended from above,
Now hold me close to your heart and breasts,
My love will be awesome and I won't be like a beast.

Your tempting lips appeared to me like fire,
And deep down I am touched with urgent desires,
Your shape is satisfying to any human eyes,
I believe you must have made many cry.

This moment I have found you my sweetheart,
You have now become my only treasured art,
I will love you and adore you today, tomorrow and forever,
And forevermore we would always be together.

Let me finally say, you are charming to behold,
So together our love would never grow old,
And upon each other we would depend,
So tomorrow, our love to the heights will ascend.

....

(71) Our secret togetherness

Our secret and beautiful togetherness,
Was wonderful, but seemed to be like madness,
Together we cuddled tightly,
Close together, we did everything quietly.
Our secret, soft and loving whispers,
Sure, at such time we felt much wiser.
This sweet loving was like an appetizer,
Along with our tender and tasty lips,
From which there were no slips,
As we together both dipped,
And with each other we really sipped.
To each other we became kinder,
As we share each other in a way that was splendor.
With respect for each other's feeling,
We didn't have to go screaming,
Because our arms together were locked,
And from side to side we both rocked,
For sure we made our togetherness a reality.
We are happy and feeling very healthy.
This secret love, so nice, tender and soft,
And really cool as sailing on a raft,
We had fun and lots of laughs.

Together we shared lots of good thoughts,
This sweet togetherness, this really felt good,
For we were really in a good mood,
And from where we both lay or stood,
So we relaxed and enjoyed lots of good food.
Secret is this love, and of course we are not bitter.
This togetherness would never whither,
For we are now feeling quite sure,
Again our togetherness is a real treasure.
Right along, our togetherness without disturbance,
But at first we had pledge that assurance,
And to this day we never altered.
Darling no way we must ever deter,
For happy is our secret love together,
And we are sure it couldn't be any better.
Remember, to start it was very secret,
And all along we kept it discreet.
And from this secret love, springs
Now, it's happiness and much joys with our rings.
This is our remembrance and contentment forever,
That now sealed our secret togetherness forever and better.

....

(72) Adore me.

Adore me now my dearest sweetheart,
So that my life could be off to a great start,
Never show me a moment of un-happiness,
I am afraid of the feelings of faintness.

Adore me truly in heart and mind,
So that I would not go to the grind,
I need your touch, the touch of love,
to give me happiness, wherever I move.

I need your heart so generous and kind,
For in you happiness I would find,
To soothe the burning desire within,
So no more would I cry or feign.

Take me now and adore me always,
I would never blush or betray,
From your charms and attitude,
For it is my desire just for you to adore me.

....

(73) Music to me.

Music to me, is like water to the thirsty throat,
Music, sweet within my soul, makes me seemed to float,
Music with all the lovely words put together,
Enlightened my life and never makes me bitter.

There are all kinds of sweet music,
Those with satisfaction, that never made anyone sick,
Other kinds of music that soothe the hearts and moods,
No wonder sweet music made me felt so good.

I need sweet music to comfort me,
When at times I felt in need to be,
For sweet music is good to heal the strains,
From many; many, lonely days in pain,

Give me music, much sweet needed music,
As lovely and tasty as the honey you lick,
What better joys in life to have,
For without sweet music, I would be feeling starved.

Good music, sweet music at times drove my soul to tears,
But most times it did cast away all my fears,

Soft sweet music with words of comfort,
That always kept my mind and feelings afloat.

I heard the sound of sweet music steep into my soul,
While I trod the lanes in quiet strolls,
Feeling real haughty, I do sing aloud,
For within myself, I felt just proud.
All music, sweet music into my body gives me content,
Such music touching me deeply to which I never relent,
Discontentment, unhappiness or problems sweet music will glorify,
If not one could be somewhat horrified.

....

(74) Dogs.

Dogs are lovely respect them as a part of life,
Some are good, some are bad, and some, would many times bites.
But a dog for sure at all times, remain a man's best friend,
and many times they are better than a friend who only pretends.

Dogs, at all times are wonderful company,
so many kept them as their only companion,
Over and around you they would always keep a watch,
Any disturbances, they would surely make a catch.

Love them adore them for they themselves do care,
So nothing about dogs, you should ever fear.
Dogs are of a different species in this world,
And many of them are also filled with curls.

They lead; they teach, guard, watch and protect you,
So just treat them well, so you would be sure,
That they would never at any time let you down,
For in every way they are your own.

With the blind they lead them perfectly everywhere,
With the children they play, but intruders they really scare,
Dogs are very good pets to love and cherish,
Just take good care of them and never let any perish.

....

(75) Glory days.

The glorious days of my beautiful life,
From the womb I came into the bright light.
I learned that I cried often and quietly,
To be lifted in mother's arms gently and lightly.

Into the arms of a mother so sweet,
As father looked on all ready to greet,
A glorious day for a wonderful son,
Whom they prayed, should have lots of fun.

Glory days on both legs and all set,
Grinning and nervously trying for my first step,
Mother looked on with her wonderful smiles,
Father ponders if I would ever walk a mile.

Glorious days with all my school mates,
Today I wonder what had become of their fate,
Those glory and wonderful days that were around,
So nice, I wish if they could again be found.

Glory days with my family, whether it's cold or hot,
Now I am enjoying them, since I am not in a cot.
With God's wonderful blessings in these days of glory,
I would always try to make those glory days, a story.

....

(76) The lost lover. (My dream.)

I recalled the hour we met my beloved,
Before such hour, I was feeling very troubled,
Now I have found a lover, so tender and soft,
And one that seemed to give me all her heart.

The true feelings of comfort came to us both,
So in our heart and minds were memories to note,
Never before, have I been so content in mind,
Until the moment I met you so sweet and kind.

I went to sleep with the feelings of happiness,
Hoping when I awoke to give you all my tenderness,
Being awake, I was alone, so I looked around,
I screamed, my lover, where can you be found.

I sat in the chair and gazed to the roof,
Where is my lover, as I sigh and wondered if I had goof,
It was just a pain to lose someone who was so lovely,
As I felt like my body was turned into a butterfly.

My heart throbbed for I was a frightened human,
And again I felt poisoned, or like a disregarded Roman
Yes! My eyes watered and my mouth filled with bubbles,
Where is my lover to relieve me of all my troubles?

I lay down with closed eyes and gazed far and wide,
I waited to see my lover so we could go for a ride.
I waited, but came no sounds, no sightings and no hints,
At such moment I felt as if I was in a clinch.

A wonderful togetherness when we met,
Now my eyes are all fluffy and wet,
Where would I find such contentment again?
Maybe I would have to go and ride the train.

Soon I realized the touch of class I had just possessed,
That I am left alone; alone and in disgust,

What did I do and where did I go wrong,
With such lover, who was so wonderfully strong?

Un-easily I went back to bed and prayed,
Although my mind and heart had all gone astray,
Again I shouted and called aloud, where is my lover,
Please, please come back and let's love again forever.

Soon I realized it was just a wonderful dream,
That caused me to blow off a lot of steam.
A restful sleep I went back to take,
I really hope that I would not dream another fake.

Now, realizing it was just a dream,
Tears came along as I steered at the beam.
My soul felt weak, as I became restless,
I prayed to be removed from such distress.

....

(77) Never look back.

Never look back to the place from where you aroused,
For there maybe obstacles that need to be disposed.
 Obstacles which could be there to ruin all your plans,
Like ambition and treasures of this glorious land.

Never look back for security or good luck,
Turning around or looking back, you could see a bad flock.
 That could discourage or spoil your schemes
From all your plans to which you had already seen.

Never look back to the impediment of success,
Look forward to the days when you could take a recess,
For sure, you will accomplish all your hopes and dreams
against all odds that could have made you lean.

Never look back on your life with any regret,
Just look forward more courageously and get set.
Move forward towards your ambition, gift or glory,
That would become forever your life story.

....

(78) A secret.

Keeping something in you privately that is called a secret,
In contact with others, you should be very discreet.
Never tell others any secret discussions,
From this there could be some repercussion.

Any secret kept in the manner told,
Must stay as it was told, no matter how old,
A secret is a trust bestowed upon you,
But only will be kept by just a few.

Never share a secret with someone else,
If you do, then you could lose yourself,
Forget a secret when others are around,
Be yourself, be real and be very sound.

Never give away a secret, for it would be a betrayal,
And it would only become a part of your denial,
To the ones who had trusted you truly,
With firmness, such secrets should only be holy.

....

(79) Young and the old.

Remember the days we were young and strong,
Doing everything, whether it was right or wrong,

We could run a race with all our energy,
And at no time, we would ever end up in a nursery.

We could and did climb the hills and mountains height,
And then down hill again where we wonder and sigh.
Energy to burn, we jumped the fences and walls,
And that was the time we had some great falls.

It was our youthful strength at its best,
So that was the time to put it to the test,
Not thinking that someday it would be lost,
To the years that come so fast.

Now old, it's what we called the golden years,
And upon our heads appeared the silver hairs,
For the energy of a wonderful life is now down,
And this is why many people frown.

To be old is no disgrace,
This is what the lucky ones will face,
From young to old, if lucky is our destiny,
That began from the hour of infinity.

But life is still wonderful for the young and elderly,
When moving fast or just going slowly,
So let's enjoy the good life, young and old,
Do it now, young and old before we unfold.

....

(80) Rich and poor.

To be poor or to be rich,
One would quickly say rich without a hitch,
Being poor, one felt as if they are in disgrace,
And this is not the fate anyone wished to face.

To be poor or even rich can breed un-happiness,
Because at times, the poor is surrounded with untidiness,
The rich filled with wealth and lots of pride,
But throughout their lives some has to hide.

Any corners of the world the poor could be fed,
But for the rich, many places they would never tread,
Because of the fear that lies within them,
It's not like the poor who may only be condemned.

What more can you gain after being rich in wealth,
When all you hope for each day is good health,
To keep you away from the poor and world's stealth,
For you never wished to feel what the poor people felt.

The poor just needed a little more and your sympathy,
Certainly that's not a big lot of treasury,
To keep them strong and with a little less strain,
Not like the rich, pushing for more to add to their gain.

....

(81) The poinsettias.

The poinsettias are such beautiful roses,
Red roses so beautiful like the model who poses.
Everyone who admire them would point their nose,
They are so pretty with smell real fresh and gorgeous.

All set in vases especially at Christmas time,
They seemed to make the home more fresh and warm,
To each and everyone, they made you feel so fine,
They are around us with such beauty and charms.

This flower so lovely, no wonder they named it the poinsettias,
All blooming lovely and shining brightly, such as

The well cooked turkey on the dining table sitting tenderly,
Cooked and ready to be devoured by the anxious mouths, timely.

The poinsettias with all its flowers so red,
What made it so red? It's water, by which it is fed,
To give it such cherished feelings of warmth,
So take a look, admire them as they could drive away all wrath.

....

(82) Never walk away from me.

Never walk away from me my friend,
Stay with me, beside me and show me your kind.
Do not walk away from me my brother,
When you are around me, I felt much better.

Do not walk away from me my sister,
I would never try to be sinister.
Sure my parents never walk away from me,
That would only break the family tie.

Don't walk away from me my lover and sweetheart,
For I have already gave you my heart.
Just love me forever, for your touch I surely need,
Just like the raindrops to the freshly sown seeds.

I love and cherish you; so I will never walk away,
And no matter what hurts me, I would just pray.
I would never walk away from the good things of life
When there's a smile, a lover or good things in sight.

Oh! I would never walk away from God the Almighty,
I will trust in him, I will walk with him and hold him tightly.
Surely I'll never walk away from life's grandeurs,
But will be strong, cool, afresh with high hopes to endure.

....

(83) The cab driver.

.The cab driver goes to bed late at nights or early mornings,
After a good rest, out again to drive and give some greetings.
To the many lovely and exciting people they would meet,
And for sure some are usually very sweet.

The cabbie, out in time to try for a good fare,
But sometimes would sit, sigh, hope and even shed a tear.
Why? Because there could be no one ready for a ride,
So he would relax, chat or take it in stride.

There are times when the lovely fares got in,
Those moments are called the lucky wins.
Lucky trips far out and into the country side,
A cabbie moving people to where they decide.

Through the heat and cold of the shifts long hours,
The cabbie winds his way like being on a tour.
Fares to destinations that made him very happy,
Not even thinking of those that made him fear in anxiety.

A cabbie drove many, many lovely fares,,
All around the city, and different places, with real cares.
To many, many places they had never known or seen,
And all that was always done for a fee.

....

(84) Weapons of war.

Many nations in this world are always at war,
For they believed their weapons are at par.

So they would fight each other with their might and will,
To boasts to the world with their mighty weapons and skills.

Weapons of wars are just dangerous ammunitions,
That's only destroys one's life, just like malnutrition,
For once attacked you could be destroyed,
Like the people who fed themselves on steroids.

Weapons of wars are very sickening to the human minds,
Just to think of the ways their uses are unkind,
For they destroyed, kill and maim,
Weapons only elevate the inventors for honor and fame.

Weapons of war are not designed for trees, bugs and flies,
But against people to strike and split the human ties,
All because of covetousness, envy or human greed,
That may elevate them in history like a lasting seed.

....

(85) I Will Wait.

Oh my darling, I waited and thought of you all through the night,
I waited, and thought of you through the lonely days,
As I waited, I wondered if I was doing things right,
And in my waiting, I felt dumb and really ignorant of what to say.

Oh darling, I am here just waiting patiently for you,
But it doesn't matter how long I have to wait,
Because you are the only one and not two,
That I would wait to cast my enticing bait.

I would be waiting through the darkness,
And I will wait in the bright sunlight,
I will wait for you even if I am placed in a harness,
Just to wait for you, for love and not a fight.

For love is sweet and love is golden,
So I have to wait for you my sweet charm,
Because to have and received love in a way that's sudden,
Sometimes, such love may never remain in my arms.

I will wait for you and your tender touch,
While the kind heart still throbs within me,
I will wait on the porch or the coach,
Just for you my lover, I'll wait for thee.

I knew my patience in waiting won't be in vain,
Not for one so wonderfully and charming.
My waiting, I pray and hope will never caused me pain,
And I hope and pray that I am not just assuming.

The distance between us, so near yet so far,
While the times to wait seemed so long,
I wish if I could fly, jump or ride to you in a car,
But since I can't, I will wait and try to keep very strong.

....

(86) A woman.

Lovely woman today who was born a baby,
Lovely you grew and so very steady,
Sweeter you become as life goes on,
So upon you will always shine the sun.

Golden days beautiful woman, you will forever enjoy,
And that will make you feel just buoyed,
You are so charming in every ways a woman could be,
Nice to know your loveliness is there for all to see.

Sure your lovely life will always be so,
And your examples also, many others will toe.

For in you as a woman all the good things exists,
From which no one can ever resist.

A lovely woman to be with all the way,
Like being on a ship heading into its bay,
To settle down in comfort and peace,
A woman is really precious in God's grace.

Keep beautiful sweet woman, for it does pay,
And your loveliness is like the sunshine rays,
Charming woman as you are is just golden,
You are beautiful as a lovely planted garden.

....

(87) I remember.

I remembered the place where I was born,
I remembered our large house; it was very, very lovely,
A beautiful lawn with many roses that adorn,
And the fence and garden were grown very thickly.

I remembered our garden alongside the pond,
With lovely vegetables, and lots of fishes from the river's catch,
Red fishes, black fishes, silver fishes to which we were really fond,
We admired those fishes in the days and in the nights with a match.

I remembered the mountains vast,
To where my eyes were always cast,
As I did admired the slopes and countryside,
Where I went and enjoyed my downhill slides.

I remembered my parent's large plantation,
Where there was lots of vegetation,
From where mother made the dishes for us all,
Such feelings that made us felt real tall.

Those glorious moments I still remembered,
As we all remember Christmas in December.
But memories in all of us, does sometimes fail,
Those wonderful memories always, with us stays.

No one could ever bring back those happy days again,
Because they are gone as yesterday's falling rain,
But i still remembered them quite well,
So today there are lots of memories to tell.

....

(89) Poverty.

This word describe all those who are in poverty,
Sure it's like the ownership of people with property.
No one ever wished for this kind of life,
But what can anyone do when things did not go right.

Poverty sinks deep into have not souls,
As lying deep in a darkened hole,
There with suffering, with torment and pain.
This is not the life anyone would ever feign.

Deep into poverty one grabs at anything,
Just to get some help for one's suffering.
Hoping that this would lead to some comfort,
And assist in one's poverty and discomfort.

When one is in poverty and very poor,
They can never even think of taking a tour.
So let's not despise those in poverty,
Help them whenever you can, to find some tranquility.

....

(89) Fall season (Canada)

The beautiful warm summer is gone again,
With just a little rain no strain and without pain.
It was wonderfully warm and pleasant,
For such time was like a wonderful present.

Fall season is here once more,
And nearly all the trees become bare,
Their green and lovely leaves of the year,
Then others start arranging their winter's gears.

The leaves are brown, some purple and some are red,
Too bad they will now have to shed,
The real beauty of leaves and flowers from their branches,
Like the cattle leaving the fields for their ranches.

The gorgeous flowers are now pale,
From which the cooler air made them frail,
Now the fallen leaves, spreads over roads and lawns,
With open eyes, one wondered if there was a storm.

Lovely green trees, now appeared to be like dead trees,
For with many trees there are no leaves to see,
A beautiful scene and another of Canada's season's beauty,
It's so real, glorious breath taking and really pretty.

....

(90) Snow.

Snow arrived in this season called winter,
On the roads, hills and tracks, really bad for sprinters,
But this is always the time of the year
This time everyone has got something to spare.

In walking, jogging and even driving,
Doing many things outside as if one was crying,
As the snow drifts shyly from the sky,
We all admire it, and sometimes even sigh.

So beautiful, one would ask, is this heavenly blessings?
Falling upon the trees, the grass and railings,
It can be like that for months and weeks,
But it never really made anyone very weak.

Because it always seemed so rare,
Beautiful it can be seen from far or near,
The snow is glorious to watch, as it falls from above,
Like herds of sheep moving in droves.

Play in it, enjoy it or even taste it,
Much of it, lots of it or even a little bit,
Snow doth beautify the trees and slopes,
As the golden chains made like ropes.

Snow is the skier's love,
Far on the hills and above,
Where they bring their gears and skis,
For all to watch the fun, and steep one's soul in bliss.

....

(91) At the end of a love affair.

As one came to the end of a love affair,
Where one thoughts was there as just perfect,
Sure it had been seen that one had shown cares,
Then suddenly something appeared that made one reflect,
This caused one to forget the moments close together,
In private plans, talks and hopes,
This made one sigh, think and hope, whether,

One could only bare it and cope.
Words spoken became lip service,
Then that feeling of one's heart does vanish.
Was this love just like a device?
That only caused the mind to be tarnish.
Your polished words seemed so divine,
Your actions were sweet like sucking honey,
And all had seemed to be fine.
So ending this love affair this quickly, seemed very funny,
Let's always talk with true honesty,
I say to everyone in this wonderful life.
Try, never to let love be a travesty,
It's better to give your tongue a bite.
Show honesty and truth always,
Let life be like the sun's rays,
That will strengthened each move we make,
It will be for our happiness and for God's sake.
Loving words spoken now seemed only false,
When in such quick moments they are forgotten,
From that, which one did not get the real taste?
If what we believe maybe real **rotten**.
A bright thank you to a lovely baby,
So if opportunity arises again, let's be ready,
May God continue to bless you in truth and in honesty.
Charming and sweet you are, so all would find you real tasty.

....

(92) Love me.

Stepping from my door my eyes first met on you,
You seemed to be one of a chosen few,
For your radiance gave me a tickle within,
With your looks, my body shakes as if I was in a rhythm.

I could see love sparkling in your eyes,
My mind wonders and my heart sighs,

Are you the lover, I found at last,
Sure, you could be the lover that was lost.

I continually dreamt of your radiance and beauty,
For you are so charming and really pretty,
And I see the tantalizing smile you possessed,
So my love and darling I feel somewhat obese.

I pray it's not just wishful thinking,
Or maybe just bells in my ears ringing,
You looked so romantic in every ways,
Tell me darling, what more can I say.

My thoughts of you gave me joys and happiness to remember,
Years around, January through to December,
As I pray our love is here to stay forever,
But to break, separate or neglect we must never

....

(93) Reach out

Reach out to those we love and love so well,
Reach out far and wide so that we can tell,
Many others have the feelings that are deep within us,
Allowing others to know and honor our trust.

Reach out to the sick and lonely,
Reach out and try to make them homely,
This would make our life beautiful in everyway,
With all we can do and have to say.

Reach out to the poor and needy,
Just reach out, and never be too greedy,
In this way happiness will always be there,
In reaching out to others, so they would feel no fear.

Reach out and be very helpful,
Reach out and be also grateful'
For someone's life needs some attention,
Just to ease a lot of their tension.

Reach out and be very honest,
Reach out to all and even those at rest,
Sure your effort will be adored,
And no one will ever be bored.

Reach out in fine spirit,
Reach out and try to visit,
Reach out, reach out and never resist,

The kindness you can do for others.
Do not sit back and say never bother,
In reaching out this will be good to your soul forever.

....

(94) Yearning for love

Are you lonely for love, or maybe yearning?
Are you dumb or sick and needed some caring?
Or for the love in your life, that could be grand?
And then find a lover, a darling, a wife or husband.

Love is something we always yearned for,
Whether we are here, there or afar,
What else is there to make our lives so happy?
With this kind of love, our lives would never be sloppy.

Yearning for love is like needing food,
Something to make the body feels real good,
For love is like food, we all really need,
So yearning for it, is wonderful indeed.

Feeling un-steady and needing something,
So right in your ears, maybe, bells are ringing,
In words of love that sounds so sweet,
Which give the heart many extra beat.

When one pines and yearned for love,
Then it's good to pray to our lord above,
Both God and love is needed that one maybe bound,
As we try to make the mind very sound.

One's yearning is sometimes not in vain,
For love sometimes comes without much strain,
And with happiness glowing in thee,
So that all in this world will want to see.

Yearn for true love then go try for it,
While you are strong and feeling fit,
And for sure we need God and love at all times,
With God and love, our lives will always be fine.

....

(95) Thanks for waiting.

(Love is a gift)

Thanks for waiting, for what we both thought had died,
You may think that all the love has gone dried,
Things do happen when some careless person,
Does something wrong to you without a reason.

You may put this precious gift like "love" aside,
Just like some who takes others for a ride,
But think of it, even if the giver seemed worthless,
In this life any experience may be a good test.

Actions like those sometimes caused others to give up,
Because it could make anyone very jealous,
But one can keep that special gift, "love" hidden,
Although in heart one could be saddened.

Never disregard the gift of love or the giver as nothing,
For in later years, happiness could be gained with something,
Its funny, good things many people don't really appreciate,
Precious things possessed, which could never depreciate.

Until it is gone, lost or never to return,
Then one would feel as if they are burnt.
Wishing it could return, pondering in regrets,
It's their fault, so they can only be silent and fret.

Just take and accept it in the first place,
Then nothing could be thrown in your face,
Because if it had no use at first,
Then never accept it just to cool your thirst.

Make good use of the gift of love today,
Accept it warmly as you accept the sunshine rays,
Because it make you smile and never frown,
Then, you may not say if you had known.

Thanks for your waiting, for this gift of love beloved,
As the aches and pains will soon be solved,
Thanks for waiting with all your patience,
Right now there will be no resistance.

....

(96) How I see love.

I see love with warmth and a true sweetness,
I see real love filled with happiness,

Love with the ecstasy of many absorbing kisses,
 All filled with satisfaction and wonderful taste.

Love with hot lips and sweet splendor,
Just so nice, satisfying and pure,
Along with the surrendering of each other's body,
This kind of love will always make anyone ready.

Love that gives contentment,
A wonderful love without any resentment,
Love, and all love are all the thoughts of you,
But it's true, such love is only reserve for a few.

True love is solid and everlasting,
When two stick together without resisting,
True love could guide us along the path of life,
With warmth and tenderness that is just so right.

True love is possessed with wonderful memories,
Just like those old time stories,
For its true that love blossoms in our hearts,
That gives us happiness and lots of treats.

True love is like springtime flowers,
Bringing comfort like been under the shower,
So no matter how muddled the mind,
Love can unwind and love can be kind,

Love is something that made us special,
Like the looks they called facial,
Love can never be old or too young,
When true love is there and is always strong.

Love and real true love can give inner peace,
And erase all the doubts we sometimes face,
Even when life seemed to be empty and dull,
With nothing left to fulfill.

Life is just beautiful when there is true love,
Feeling sure that such love is sent from above,
To be shared and enjoyed tenderly with each other,
At this time, into tomorrow and forever.

....

(97) Discouragements

In this world and in this life God gave to us,
So in him, let us pray and placed our trust,
Creating us he, he was never discouraged for he had hopes,
So he devoted all his time; and alone he coped.

So in this life we all find discouragements,
To mar our days and most of our moments,
These could be simple or sometimes great,
But let's look at God, and keep the faith.

Being discouraged even if we felt really down,
Just remember this, we, God will never disown,
Because he brought us into this beautiful world,
So with faith he would help us to be bold.

God is with us, so let us feel encouraged,
Our sins we pray to him, he would surely purged,
At times, down and discouraged as we may be,
Just look to god and for sure he would see.

In this life discouragements are bound to arise,
To all of us, and not only to those who cries,
This is the way for us all,
Until the day we receive his call.

When discouragements comes, never give up,
Keep on trying and praying without a stop,

This is what our lives are all about,
So to give up, for sure you would be in doubt.

Discouragements weakened the strong and the weak,
That could placed one in a mood never to speak,
But it could be overcome if one is strong,
That is true, those words are not wrong.

When we are discouraged, we must seek God first,
Before our minds doth get worse,
When God is with us, then all is well,
In him we trust, and in him our faith must dwell.

With every discouragement, one can overcome,
So in the glories of happiness one would roam,
For god brought us here from the beginning,
Discouraged or not, in him we would always be rejoicing.

....

(98) Be happy with yourself.

Many may look at you with scorn, and then wonder,
Which make you sigh and cause your mind to wander,
Why does people behaved so foolish?
Because, even children wouldn't be so childish,

One must love and enjoy his or her life in happiness,
And be always gay and in true loveliness,
Happy with cleanliness and enhance your life with pride,
As in each day you happily glide.

Always keep your smiles, your pleasantness and charms,
That makes your sweet life so nice and warm,
Make yourself happy and always be very clean,
This is a glorious way one must always be seen.

Never worry about comments or one's disregard,
In your heart it could make things very hard,
Keep your head high, and with difficulties just smile,
And pray you would go a million extra miles.

Plan your way to be very content and happy,
Forget and ignore all those who think you are sloppy,
You are beautiful to yourself and many others too,
So consider yourself charming, handsome, happy and true.

Remember this world is a beautiful place,
Try to smile at the insults you would always face,
In your honesty, just live the best of today,
So tomorrow you could have lots more to say.

Why, worry, and worry and worry,
This could someday make you real sorry,
Understand yourself and do things right,
So that the dirt and insults could fades from your sight.

One should always take good care of themselves, it's a blessing,
Like a good band-aid, such a perfect dressing,
That soothes the blisters, and gives you contentment and happiness,
Just be happy with yourself, and without any sadness.

....

(99) War remembrance.

Those wars were fought with velocity,
In them there was a lot of electricity.
In God the nation had prayed always,
That the soldiers would never betray.

To the hills, valleys and sky they looked,
All from the sea shores where they stood.

From the valleys they all together unite,
All united before they started to fly like a kite.

They were soldiers in battles to win,
So in the eyes of God there was no sin.
Fighting for their country and people's freedom,
As all prayed that none would be doomed.

Thank God for this our wonderful country,
A land we all claimed as our bounty.
A sweet life we are enjoying, after those fighting days,
Safe soldiers home all the countries prays,

To heaven there were prayers for those who were lost,
So at this moment all should pray and show some cares.
Let's all pray for soldiers who took their places,
For our country; so bravely they showed their faces.

To all soldier, we all pray that the world would honor you,
All brave soldiers who took the oath to be true.
Defending all human rights to be free and proud,
No matter how rough and unruly was the crowd.

....

(100) The warmth, of a lover.

We met, shook hands with a warm embrace,
Talking for a while, we got to the point,
That there was no barrier we could trace,
No matter how far we looked at our joint.

We hugged, squeezed with kisses to the cheeks,
Sure we wasn't doing anything out of sight,
It seemed our love has already reached the peak,
Sure, our warm exchanges were really bright.

We shared kisses so warm and tender,
Whether hot love or warm love, it was enjoyable,
Because each of us was enjoying real splendor,
We embraced and found each other feasibly.

Yes! This is the true feelings with all lovers,
This warm love has given us the joys of life, so
As love blossomed, over yonder we will tower,
Energetic, happy, loving and sharp like a knife..

Let this warm love be stable forever,
As we learn more and more of each other.
A great reward, as we build this love stronger,
From the hour we met as strangers.

No other love and lover will be so warm,
For within ourselves, we will only see charms.
Let's stay as happy and true warm lovers,
Very soon and timely we'll move to the covers.

....

(101) Burdens in this life.

The burdens of life, we all encounter today,
Must not in any way make us feel to stray.
We all must struggle, and fight these burdens,
Calmly, and patiently, and avoid going too suddenly.

Life can be a real burden that made us, think only of surviving,
In this world where almost everyone are always singing,
Living; working, and enjoying real happiness,
Burdens are there to take up and carry in gentleness..

Sometimes there are burdens, with even those you trust,
As they would at times drives you into disgust.

These burdens come to us in sleeping, and in a dream,
So in walking; talking, and ponder, we even sometimes scream.

No matter where you are, there are burdens around,
That makes the mind and heart felt as if you are bound.
There are burdens to the trees; insects, and animals,
Burdens are with us that would always be our trials.

Keep in mind we are not saints, but sinners all,
So burdens could someday, make us fall.
None of us are free from burden or problems,
Because they are with us, from top, centre, and bottom.

We all must pray to GOD; in-order to be burden free,
So, that we could look afar and see,
And in seeing our-selves, a burden free world,
Living, loving, and enjoying it as diamonds, pearls or gold.

35 Quotes

"Thirty five quotes"

1) Please remember that it is your enemy who you are always knowledgeable of; always on the lookout for and in doubt of. But with some friends, whom you called true friends, always be scared, be fearful and be very much concerned.

2) The way in which I used my energy is the way in which I feel my strength.

3) Riches are not my desires, but love, understanding, good health, contentment and happiness which make my days and years so bright.

4) Trust not certain close friends, for they are the ones that will remove the chair which you are about to sit on.

5) Never let the overnight strains and disappointments conquer your faith and confidence. Ignore and try to forget it, so that tomorrow you will rise with more faith and confidence in yourself.

6) There are times when loud mouths will blast your ears, play deaf, say something different or even sing a song.

7) Whenever the devil encounters you, look up to the sky and sigh, even if you don't pray.

8) Your words are like a hard punch that sucks deep. To retaliate, I may be too cruel, so I will play dumb and hold my tongue.

9) You seemed to possess such touch of class that maybe you are able to crush a rock. For my body nervously shakes, my knees seemed to be weakening with you in my sight.

10) Press me forward, then press me backward, what comes out of me, that's me, so if you like it, that's yours to keep forever.

11) The goals of life seemed to be very easy, but to get them, one has to try and work very hard, because discouragements may even mar your pathway. To give up may be cowardly, so plunge forward bravely and courageously, for sure you would succeed.

12) Love and really true love is like a glass of good fresh milk. Preserve it, and it would last forever and forever. Meddle or tamper with it, then it becomes foul, it stinks, and would have to be cast away.

13) All adults should blossom and bare fruits for harvest, so that their children can pick, eat and enjoy the very best in their years ahead.

14) My eyes have just seen the face of a true love. Where were you? Or was it that I could not see before.

15) Let me find a mate,
In whom I may have some faith,
So we could be lovers,
Sometimes in the future, but we must be clever.

16) I felt the touch of your fingers as they stimulates my nature, rekindles my flesh, and sets me a flame like the burning fire.

17) Whisper my name silently in your mind. Call me frequently in thoughts and even out of the dark, for in the name of true love I would appear.

18) Be careful never stick your nose into other people's face. You may have to withdraw wet and slimy.

19) If your dignity is tainted, your honor suppressed and your freedom taken away, just keep your mentality perfect. You will need it when all has been returned.

20) The charms of your sweet life seemed to melt my cold blood, the very moment I set my eyes on you.

21) Your warmth, your kindness and your patience can win my love and not your beauty or handsomeness.

22) What a voice, just roaring like thunder, a behavior so sharp and rough like a splintered bottle. I think some reshaping maybe needed.

23) It seems that there are many wicked thoughts sinking into you deeper and deeper, like the worm protruding into the earth.

24) The principles of life must never be only hoping thoughts, but they must be the goal of life.

25) Now is the moment that the truth doth flow freely as water from the open tap, so who else could speak it better than you did.

26) True or false, but this is it; to have a lot of money will enable your children to keep in contact with you at all times.

27) The cold mornings chill my bones,
The dull faces drove my spirit cold,
Happiness is like the breath of fresh air so sweet,
But where is the sun that could make it a treat.

28) In order to get a thank you or a hello from certain people in this life, one will have to do something very good to them, like the sun which shines gloriously on them for a smile.

29) Good deeds can make real friends, and at times it may even spoil friendship. Just the way money made good friends and break good friendship.

30) Twist not your tongue for your desires, because it could be twisted on you by someone else in a more sneaky way.

31) Never beg, never steal and never subordinate. Be content with the little you have and try to be satisfied, and you will have a better and more independent life style.

32) Power, boasts, ignorance and greed can sometimes instigate troubles, violence and wars.

33) Never be an informant. First think of your conscience, then think of the memories after. Information may be good at times, and at other times hurt someone, and that could live with you forever. So, information to others, that may hurt, never, never does.

34) Never erode a person's rights to satisfy your own greed, or to enhance your own ambition.

35) I am now an adult person, not to be gagged by my own parents, my wife/husband, my children, my friends or someone like you. I will speak my mind freely without reservations and with a clear and clean conscience.

52 Short Verses

Double alphabet in short verses.

Fifty-two short verses which either begins with or is followed with the letters of the alphabet.

....

1A)   I know we are far apart,
      But a taste of true love we both felt,
      Attributed to the way we did start,
      Along the way, let's make it more real.

2A)   Astray I thought, as I walked the alleyway,
      Amidst the flowers so beautiful,
      All green leaves lined the pathway,
      And around were flowers so beautiful.

1B)   Bewildered I felt my darling,
      Because I felt as if were falling.
      Bring to me now, something very precious,
      Before I lose what I think was delicious.

2B)   Better to be in love than to hate,
      Because life is just too sweet,
      Berate no one for God's sake,
      Because it's best to give everyone a real treat.

1C)   Come hold me my lovely baby,
      Close to me you should always be,

Call me by my name sweetheart,
Charming you is in my thoughts.

2C) Count the days of our lives,
Consider the dilemma that we may encounter,
Careful planning without any strife,
Coming close together there was no dissenter.

1D) Direct my life, oh my Lord forevermore,
I will not distance myself from thee,
Days of my life, I will pray to you for sure,
I thank you Lord for all you gave to me.

2D) Darling forever my dear,
Don't you know there's nothing to fear?
Do, please come and be beside me,
The door to my heart is opens for you to see.

1E) I see your eyes so bright and lovely,
Each time I looked at you,
Every time, every where, weekly or daily,
Everlastingly lovely, you seemed to be so true.

2E) In each hour that I pray,
Expecting sometimes miracles,
Even though nothing may,
Either falls from above or from a pinnacle.

1F)   Far away from the good things of life,
      For me it's no real big deal.
      I am okay and feeling al-right,
      But further down I will have more zeal.

2F)   Forever and a day you will always be mine,
      For upon your body, I hope to dine,
      Free from all worries I am so content,
      Face to face, you, I would never resent.

1G)   Gaming is not a part of our affair,
      Gone or all fears, so now it's real care,
      Good times must be with us, two,
      Glad is my heart, so forever this love is true.

2G)   Grand, we would called this good life of ours,
      Great is our God, who made us all,
      Give me your hand, let's together show favors,
      And glorify all without getting a fall.

1H)   Happy times are here again,
      Having such good togetherness with friends,
      And hoping this friendliness will sustain,
      Hesitating I would not, because of the trend.

2H)   How long must I continue to wait?
      In-order to have you in my arms,
      Holding you close, and in all good faith,
      Saying, here is my darling with all her charms.

1I) Impress me with your wisdom,
Even with imaginations of your dreams,
Impart from you, I would never throughout this kingdom,
For images of you would always be on my screen.

2I) I must hold you now and kiss you my dear,
For ivory seemed to paint your lips,
Interested you seemed to be, so I do care,
As I always idolize the spring-like tulips.

1J) Just at this moment we felt for each other,
The juices of love begins to flow,
Jokes and riddles we put together,
Joining hands as the lights seemed to glow.

2J) Join your hands with mine, you sweet little damsel,
Jilt each other not, as we felt this tenderness,
Juggling in our hearts, our minds and our fancies,
Jokingly we chide each other because of nervousness.

1K) Kiss me now, until the day is done,
Knight me with the sweat of your brow,
That I would knuckle right down,
To kindle thee, and be like the cock that crows.

2K) Kiss me and touch me my lovely baby,
The key to my heart is yours my sweet beau,
Keep me forever, for I am prepared and ready,
I will kindle my love and affection for you.

1L)   Lie beside me my one and only dearest,
        Let's make love and show all our cares,
        Loveliness between us without any fears,
        As the living light will show you are the sweetest.

2L)   Let thy love be sweeter than honey, sweet bunny,
        Loosened not, your grip upon me,
        Love lost could appear to others very funny,
        Like a dirty rag hanging from a tree.

1M)   Most of my years have now been spent,
        Meeting lots of people, even those in tents,
        Good morning, hello, a good way to greet,
        Much more will I give love, even at your feet.

2M)   Make me your darling and beloved friend,
        As my eyes looked on you, I do understand,
        In making a friendship true and golden,
        A mirror of love came so sudden.

1N)   Now that we have fallen for each other,
        None of us must ever change or differ,
        Never fuss, fight or wither,
        Noting our togetherness will be much better.

2N)   No one or nothing can take your place,
        No matter what may be given or seen anew,
        For never will I ever try to deface,
        Nor distance myself from you.

1O) Open your heart to all who needs it,
Offering warmth, kindness and tenderness,
Offend none, not even the misfits,
Over you, God will place all the happiness.

2O) Come over here you lovely sweetheart,
Let's put our hands to each other's heart,
Overnight we both can stare towards the sea,
Often times there may be lots to see.

1P) Precious moment we spent together,
Praying we must, that our lives will be better,
Let's not ponder about the future or weather,
Promises we made will hold and make us sweeter.

2P) Play with me, for I surely need some encouragements
Place your hand upon me and I will be happy,
Pleasurable moments, without any resentment,
Politeness I possess, so I would never act shabby.

1Q) Am I qualified to be your mate?
Quaint feelings got to me as I passed by,
I question myself in good faith,
Before I quash such feelings and just sigh.

2Q) Quiet, but not so often we sometimes find,
Quick sweet love that can be so kind,
Quoting lovely verses to each other's desires,
Quietly I would do so before we retire.

1R) Riddle my life with words precious as gold,
Remember I had loved all that was told,
Respect for each other without reservation,
Resistance we must to all temptations

2R) Reach out to all others my good friends,
Respond to others with love and eagerness,
Feel relieved that we are God sent,
Render help in everyway and show unselfishness.

1S) Sustain me with your love always,
Like a sheep sitting in my pathway,
Such experiences made me felt as if I am falling,
I swallowed swiftly as I kept on sighing.

2S) Sample me with the world of sweet kisses,
Satisfy me now with all your caresses,
Say, forever I would always be cherished,
Sweet love I need, that must never diminish.

1T) Talented you are in the challenging world,
Tempting to the stones you was, that lay mute,
Taunt me just like the glistening pearls,
Take me and play with me like a flute.

2T) Tarnish my life, but not with ugly un-truths,
Turn away from me, for you maybe a brute,
Teased me hungrily with love un-ending,
Teach me more, so that I may be better in bending.

1U)   Like an umbrella, under you I will find some shade,
      Un-affected from the problems all around,
      Under no circumstances let me fade,
      The union between us must be true and sound.

2U)   Unable to sleep as I dream of you,
      Unlike others I am true and pure,
      Unfair it may seemed, but I wish to stay,
      Up or down I am yours in all the days.

1V)   Victorious I was in my adventures,
      My voice and words sweetly flowing,
      From my vocal cord, I ventured without denture,
      Very, very lovely songs, like a choir singing.

2V)   Valid was my time spent in reading,
      A variety of topics which gave me joys,
      Valentine day I enjoyed all my writings,
      Various ideas gained, will not vanish like toys.

1W)   I am waiting to hear you say,
      Will you one day walk with me on the beach
      With many wishes for our future love plays,
      Wondering if it's the top we have reached.

2W)   I wish for a lover and a true one too,
      To whom I would quickly woo,
      With all my love and cares, eternally,
      With you I should be fit, physically.

1X) X-rays always is a part of our lives,
    So exercise restraint in our affairs,
    Take extra caution in avoiding all strife,
    While excelling in wisdom and showing cares.

2X) Expose me to all good things of progress,
    Examples that I could show to others,
    Exempting me from all distress,
    For I must express myself with more cares.

1Y) Yesterday we met and talked with much admiration,
    Your conversation was very much inspiring,
    Oh yes! Youth was out of imagination,
    Let's yearn for more, as it was so intriguing.

2Y) Youthful days we all enjoyed,
    Young we were, when we could see no evil,
    Yes! It is true we both felt happy,
    As we yearn for more and try to be civil.

1Z) Zephyr may describe our love, tender and so cool,
    Zealousness appears as we dipped into the pool,
    No zero love between us as it would be forever and a day,
    Zip! It's like a sound I heard saying, let's not betray.

2Z) A zigzag way of life I do not admire,
    Only zinc does perform in that way,
    I saw a zipper went by appearing like a fire.
    From zone to zone it went, and into a bay.

About the Author

My name is Hubert Winston Anderson. I am the third eldest in a family of six, and that is four boys and two girls. Because I always loved and enjoyed reading and writing, I devoted a lot of my spare time just to do so in the reading of Biblical stories, historical books, fiction, non-fiction and good old story books, and of course magazines and news print.

As I moved about my business in life, I always have with me my pen and a pocket book, where I scribble all the little thoughts and ideas that blossomed in my mind. At some later date I would sit down, relax my mind and make those lines into more interesting readings, and this is why I was able to compile all these poems, verses and quotes.

My schooling was grade eleven, and from there I went into the police force then did some travels working at many jobs. I took a course in bookkeeping with the London school of Business from where I received a certificate in book-keeping.

While I was at school and in grade seven, I penned this little poem, and of course was given high marks by my teacher.

>Smoking<

Cigarette or tobacco to me is a nasty weed,
The devil is the only person or idiot to sow the seed,
Because, tobacco only picks your pocket and burn your clothes,
Furthermore its smokes just make a chimney of your nose.

My teacher who did not smoke and who really dislike people who smoke was very proud of me, so my poem was displayed in the school. From such time I really felt inspired to write my own poems some day.

I hope and trust you will enjoy reading these poems, as I have another book of poems that I hope will be on the market very soon.

Thanks,
Hubert Winston Anderson

Printed in the United States
89543LV00003B/52-120/A